Flower, Song, Dance
Aztec and Mayan Poetry

Flower, Song, Dance

Aztec and Mayan Poetry

Translated by
David Bowles

LAMAR UNIVERSITY press

ISBN: 978-0-9852552-8-2
Library of Congress Control Number: 2013942230

Illustrated by Nicol Bowles
Cover art by Noé Vela
Manufactured in the United States of America

Lamar University Press
Beaumont, Texas

For

Jan Seale

whose encouragement
made this project
possible.

David Bowles' published books include
  Mexican Bestiary (with Noé Vela)
  The Seed: Stories from the River's Edge (with Angélica
     Maldonado)
  The Blue-Spangled Blue
  The Deepest Green
  The Rising Red
He has also edited several books:
  *Along the River: An Anthology of Voices from the Río
     Grande Valley*
  Along the River 2: More Voices from the Río Grande
  Donna Hooks Fletcher: Life and Writings
He has published poetry and short fiction in a number of
journals and anthologies, including *Twenty Pasta, Poetry
& Vino Chapbook, Eye to the Telescope, Gallery, Out of the
Gutter Online, Juventud! Growing up on the Border, The
Monitor, BorderSenses,* and *Translation Review.*

Jaguar Flower

Other books from Lamar University Press include

Alan Berecka, *With Our Baggage*
Jeffrey DeLotto, *Voices Writ in Sand*
Mimi Ferebee, *Wildfires and Atmospheric Memories*
Michelle Hartman, *Disenchanted and Disgruntled*
Gretchen Johnson, *The Joy of Deception*
Tom Mack and Andrew Geyer, editors, *A Shared Voice*
Dave Oliphant, *The Pilgrimage*
Harold Raley, *Louisiana Rogue*
Jan Seale, *Appearances*

www.LamarUniversityPress.Org

Acknowledgments

A book like the one you hold in your hands should never be considered the effort of a single person. I am primarily grateful to the work of Ángel María Garibay Kintana, Miguel León-Portillo, John Bierhorst, Willard Gingerich and, and David Bolles, whose scholarly trailblazing made walking these linguistic trails easier. The community of poets in the Río Grande Valley has been my moral support through the long months of translation: a heartfelt thanks to Edward Vidaurre, Rachel Vela, Alan Oak and all the rest of the Poetry, Pasta & Vino and We Need Words folks for allowing me to try out versions of these poems at readings they organized. Amado Balderas, José Chapa, Erika Garza-Johnson, and Katie Hoerth—les debo un montón.

Many scholarly discussions buoyed my efforts to craft viable poetic translations. Dr. Steven Schneider, Dr. Rob Johnson, Dr. René Saldaña, Jr., and Dr. José María Martínez indulged me in all manner of conversations about issues I faced during the project. Their positive feedback and learned guidance was crucial to its completion. Rossy Lima Padilla's beautiful Nahuatl and unerring sense of musicality aided me in finding a voice that would do some justice to the originals. Tlazohcāmati huel miyac!

The visual arts have always been a great source of inspiration, and I was blessed to have both Noé Vela and Nicol Bowles working with me, providing the cover and interior illustrations, respectively. Like the scribes of pre-Colombian times, they painted a world to life for me. The work of many poets also influenced me stylistically, including Seamus Heaney, Ted Hughes, Robert Frost, Maya Angelou, Annie Finch, Carmen Tafolla, Benjamín Alire Sáenz (among others). Possibly the most significant literary mentor for this endeavor has been Robert Fagles, whose masterful translations of Greek and Roman verse I revisit again and again like the most faithful of old friends.

A good number of writers extended friendship and encouragement when I needed them most, so I will express my deep gratitude to Jason Henderson, Guadalupe García McCall, Xavier Garza, Carmen Tafolla, and David Rice. Also invaluable was the support and interest of Brenda Nettles Riojas, whose *Corazón Bilingüe* radio program allows so many south Texas voices to be heard. Most important for this volume, of course, was the inimitable 2012 Poet Laureate Jan Seale, who asked to read my very first translated Nahuatl poem and then convinced me to do more. I will always cherish her gift of friendship.

As ever, the primary inspiration for everything I do is my beautiful family: my kids—Angelo, Char and Nikki—and my wonderful wife Angélica. Son mi flor, mi canto, mi danza eterna. Los quiero con toda el alma.

CONTENTS

Illustrations

Introduction

As far as we can determine, song and dance were as integral a part of the lives of ancient Mexican peoples as they are today. From religious ritual to broad comic satire, Mayan and Aztec verse was written by and for human beings very much like us, driven by the same needs and fears. Much of the literature of pre-Columbian Mesoamerica has been lost to us, however, victim of conquest and time. Ironically, most of the indigenous verse that we still possess was preserved by the ethnographic work of Catholic priests like Bernardino de Sahagún, who recorded the traditions and songs of native Mexicans years after the Aztec Triple Alliance had fallen to Spain. Of course, the selective nature of their codices and the clear influence of Catholicism on the texts make a wholly reliable cross-section of Mesoamerican literature nearly impossible, but we have at least a reasonable approximation. The present collection seeks to give the casual reader a feel for the poetry of the Mayan and Aztec cultures by drawing on those codices, translating selected pieces with language that preserves the timeless power of their images and the emotions they evoke.

The People

In additional to its universal human appeal, of course, Meso-american poetry contains culturally specific ideas and symbols that may put off the casual reader. It is important when engaging with these texts to have a degree of context to help grapple with unfamiliar responses to the universe.

The World Tree and Networks of Power. In Mesoamerican cosmology, an *axis mundi* traversed the heavens, the earth, and the underworld. This World Tree both connected and delineated the realms, establishing *malinalli* or networks of sacred energy (called *ku* by the Mayans and *teotl* by the Aztecs) that flowed among them. In the uppermost branches of the World Tree was *Omeyocan*, abode of the dual god from whom the other deities (and by some accounts the entire universe) emanated. Another twelve celestial layers lay beneath it, home to various gods or heavenly phenomenon. Next came the earth, ringed by the cosmic sea. Below it, entwined in the roots of the World Tree, loomed the nine-layered Land of the Dead, destination of most humans upon their demise, where a four-year journey through ghastly trials purified the soul till it was ready to return to its source.

Combat and Sacrifice. For the indigenous cultures of Mexico, the world was a product of great struggle, trial and error, sacrifice. They would see our present age as either the fourth or fifth—the previous worlds having been wiped out either as failed experiments by the gods or because of strife among those deities concerning how sentient beings should look and behave as well as what crops would best sustain them. These disagreements were cataclysmic, resulting in floods, fires, and storms that razed life from our world and blotted the sun from the sky.

After the last apocalyptic event, humanity was created. But that was not enough. The Aztecs relate how all the gods came together in the darkness and built a great fire. It was clear to them that the world *must* have a sun, and the only way to bring it back into existence was for one of their number to sacrifice himself. Tecuciztecatl, a young braggart, insisted he be given the honor; each time he approached that blaze, however, he retreated in fear. Finally Nanoatzin, the oldest and weakest among them, simply stood and stepped into the fire. Tecuciztecatl, overcome with shame, threw himself after the old god. Two lights began to shine upon the horizon not long afterward; the gods hurled a rabbit at Tecuciztecatl to dim his glow. Thus were the sun and moon born out of both willing and unwilling sacrifice.

But the sun, the Aztecs tell us, could not blaze a path across the sky. The gods sat and watched it wobble redly on the horizon. Then Quetzalcoatl, the Feathered Serpent, creator of humanity, understood the true price of giving his children light: all the remaining gods would have to offer themselves up in sacrifice in order to set the sun in motion. They agreed, and he killed each and every one of them, releasing their essential sacredness. Drawing this energy into himself, Quetzalcoatl, in his aspect of Ehecatl, god of the wind, released a gale of divine power at the sun, jumpstarting its climb to zenith.

This initial sacrifice underlies a great deal of Mesoamerican religious practice. Resplendent, the sun pours *teotl* down on the world; from the day of our birth, we absorb this sacredness. It permeates our blood, our hearts, our brains. And out of respect and reciprocity toward the gods for their eternal gift, we are expected to offer them songs, dances, rites...and, if need be, our lives. Blood has to be spilled to nourish the sun, priests declared. For millennia, Mesoamericans practiced various sorts of bloodletting, spilling their own essential fluid to help ensure the daily renewal of the sun, the constant cycle of the seasons, the wheeling of the constellations through the heavens. Elaborate calendars were developed to track these cosmic patterns and to mark the important times of reciprocity with the gods. And, over the years, greater sacrifice became the norm. During centuries, volunteers and captives alike were sacrificed, their hearts removed to facilitate the return of *teotl* to its source.

Warfare in such a world view became a tool of obedience and reciprocity. As had the gods during the first four ages of the world, the city-states of Mexico clashed in armed conflict, their warriors trained to view death on the battlefield as an honorable, desirable end, followed closely by capture and ceremonial sacrifice by the opposing side. The Aztec Triple Alliance established a specific kind of pre- arranged battle called *xochiyaoyotl* or *flowery war* for the specific purpose of exchanging sacrificial victims with tributary nations via stylized combat. A code of ethics emerged, a deep-seated sense of duty that rivaled the *areté* of the Greek warrior (as expressed in the *Iliad*), the *dharma* of the Hindu *kshatriya* (seen in the epics *Ramayana* and *Mahabharata*) or the *pietas* of the Roman soldier (demonstrated by Aeneas in Virgil's timeless poem).

Rather than an eternity in Elysium Fields or freedom from rebirth, battle death for the Aztec warrior meant transformation into a companion of the sun, an embodiment of the power of movement (usually in the form of butterflies and hummingbirds). Slain warriors would assist the sun as it rose to its zenith, then return to the flowery paradise in the east to await the daily renewal of their master. They were sustained by the songs and praise of their brothers on earth, whose own music was inspired by the heavenly host in a sort of feedback loop. The maximum expression of this code was in the songs of the *tlamatinime* or philosopher-poets of the Nahua tribes who arrived in central Mexico around 500 CE, bringing their god of war Huitzilopochtli into the existing Mesoamerican pantheon and forging the cultural synthesis that would give birth to the Aztec Triple Alliance. The *tlamatinime* were normally of noble birth and studied in specialized schools called *calmecacs*. Many of them rose to be kings or military commanders. Interestingly, their power and learning opened the door to doubts. Perhaps they began to see their religious rituals were often used for political manipulation. Like Arjuna, hesitating on the battlefield in the *Bhagavad Gita*, the philosopher-poets explored their misgivings, most of them ultimately finding their faith strengthened by the process. Their work makes up the bulk of the poems in the present collection.

The Codices

Songs of Mexico. The codex known as *Cantares Mexicanos* is the largest collection of Mesoamerican verse available to us. It consists of 85 folios on which 91 songs were compiled in Nahuatl somewhere around 1585. These *cuicatl* or songs range widely in genre, from ecstatic hymns celebrating humanity's reciprocal relationship with heaven to historical ballads, bawdy satire, and philosophical musings. Glosses abound in a different hand, often trying to spin the mention of native deity into a reference to the Christian god.

Ballads of the Lords of New Spain. The codex called *Romances de los señores de la Nueva España* consists of 42 folios on which 36 songs were compiled in Nahuatl somewhere around 1582, a date attested in the *Relación* of Juan Bautista de Pomar, which was attached to the collection. These *cuicatl* are of a particular genre called *netotiliztli*: orally composed ballads that praise the deeds of great figures of the past and that were accompanied by elaborate dances. About a dozen of these *netotiliztli* also appear in slightly different form in *Songs of Mexico*. The pieces selected by the compiler of the codex are mainly from the city-state of Texcoco, a member of the Triple Alliance whose legendary ruler Nezahualcoyotl was famed as one of the greatest *tlamatini* ever.

Songs of Dzitbalché. Discovered in 1942, the codex now titled *Los cantares de Dzitbalché* contains virtually all the surviving lyrical poetry of the Mayan civilization. This document reflects many of the same rituals and religious mysticism outlined in the *Books of Chilam Balam*, compendiums of important lore from the Mayan cities of the

Yucatan peninsula. The only extant copy of the *Songs of Dzitbalché* was written in Yucatec Mayan using the Roman alphabet not long after the year 1742 by Ah Bam, an elder of the town of Dzitbalché. Many of the poems appear to be much older than the manuscript (in which Ah Bam claims a composition date of 1440 CE), especially given the descriptions of pre-Colombian rituals. As with the Aztec codices, this collection of verse was most likely transmitted orally for generations before being written down.

The Translation

The Rationale. This book stems from my fascination with Mesoamerican mythology and literature and my love of Nahuatl, the language of the people we now call Aztecs. While digging into sources for other projects, I began to realize that an accessible English poetic translation of Aztec and Mayan verse does not really exist. The codices I draw from languished untranslated for hundreds of years before scholars in the 20th century began to rise to the challenge. Angel María Garibay managed to craft Spanish versions of all of *Ballads* and most of *Songs of Mexico* before his death, and Miguel León-Portilla continued adapting those manuscripts and others, eventually creating English versions of some. Alfredo Barrera Vásquez, much like Garibay, released paleographic transcriptions and well researched scholarly Spanish translations of *Songs of Dzitbalché* in 1965.

English-language work in Mesoamerican poetry lies largely in the shadow of Thelma D. Sullivan, whose scholarly exploration of Nahuatl verse set the standard. In recent years, John Bierhorst has produced impressive paleographic editions of both *Ballads* and *Songs of Mexico,* though some of his interpretive and translation choices have stirred controversy. Several other scholars, including Earl and Sylvia Shorris, have translated select pieces from the codices. Munro S. Edmonson produced an English-language *Songs of Dzitbalché* in 1982. Even more recently, writer John Curl has produced English versions of some Mesoamerican poetry that hew close to Garibay and Vásquez, and poets like Peter Everwine have composed loose interpretations.

Most of the experts undertaking such projects are linguists, historians, anthropologists and philosophers; arguably no serious attempt has been made by a poet to craft English versions of this corpus that attempt to recreate with the tools of modern verse the feel and impact of the originals. To preserve the literal meaning of the Nahuatl or Mayan, translators have no choice but to strip away all the rhythms and musicality of the original language, little of which is transferable directly to English anyway. As a result, a reader fluent in English will have the gist of a given song, but none of the magic. While such a state of affairs is acceptable for scholarly work, there seems to be a need for translations that will appeal to the casual reader. At the urging of Texas Poet Laureate Jan Seale, I began working to help fill that gap.

Like the multiple versions of the *Odyssey,* the *Ramayana* and other important works of literature, I believe that there is room for many different takes on these important poems. The songs themselves, as I have mentioned, were orally composed to be performed, accompanied by dancing, in public settings. Different versions of the same songs exist in *Ballads* and *Songs of Mexico,* suggesting that, like European and African bards, Mesoamerican singers used mnemonic and structural devices to recreate songs on the fly at each performance, often tweaking lines and phrasings. As a result, the differences among English-language iterations should be accepted and celebrated.

Features of Mesoamerican Verse. Though replete with devices we recognize (repetitions, kennings, metaphor and simile, alliteration), Mesoamerican poetry did not follow the same sorts of prosodic customs as much traditional Western verse. Rhyme was used, but not in any perceivable scheme. As for meter, many poems tended to have lines of about 4 beats and 8 to 10 syllables, but others had longer lines, and many alternated long and short lines without discernible patterns. Stanzas were of varying length and often indicated refrains, especially in *netotiliztli,* which tend to have patterns of eight stanzas. As a result, many translators have dispensed with prosody and employed free verse as the most flexible format. Interestingly, however, we know most existing poems were set to music and accompanied by dance. In fact, some of the Nahuatl poems actually indicate what drumming pattern was to be used to accompany the singing (though scholars have still not fully deciphered the system of notation).

A Musician and Poet's Approach to Translating. Having written a good number of poems/songs and having performed them before audiences many, many times, I found it meaningful when crafting my versions to use some basic rhythmic scheme (while allowing myself absolute freedom on other matters of prosody). This basically boils down to setting a number of beats per line (anywhere from two to five), and then building around that pattern, opting for a more trochaic rhythm when I want to evoke dance, playing with dactyls for the headlong rush of war, or laying out iambic roll for more conversational reflection.

Following the lead of translators like Robert Fagles, I have tried to strike a balance between the features of the original Nahuatl or Mayan performance and the expectations of modern readers of poetry. My versions, I hope, avoid the trap of being so literal as to overwhelm my own voice or so literary that the direct power of the originals is diluted. Given the broad range of topics and poetic genres, I have tried to modulate my voice, casting it in the right tone to thread among humble praise, transporting ecstasy, berserking battle lust, agonizing doubt, and resigned acceptance. I have also worked to convey the difference between the less complex, community-centered voices of Mayan verse and the broad, bigger-than-life Nahuatl ones. If only as an echo, I hope I have preserved them for the reader's ear.

One of the most challenging aspects of this project has been working with heavily repeated words or phrases. I have avoided slavishly rendering these in the same way unless to create unity across several texts. For the Nahuatl word *xochitl*, for example, I have used *flower, blossom, bloom, bud* and other synonyms as alliteration and meter suggest. But I have in contrast translated *Ximoayan* as *Place of the Shorn* every time it appears.

Ultimately, every translator makes a given work his own, giving life to that which he can see in the piece, what he has the power to translate. When working with these powerful texts, I was struck by the epiphany that much of my interests, study and experience had built up to precisely this project. I hope that the flowers I have pulled from the vast fields of the past will, in some small way, touch you and help you to see the nearly overwhelming, tragic beauty of a world forever lost to us.

David Bowles
Río Grande Valley

Nahui Ollin

Poems from *Songs of Mexico*

The original title of this piece is "Cuicapeuhcayotl" or "song-beginning," often rendered "the origin of the songs." The reader should note that the Mexica and other Nahua tribes (now collectively known as the Aztecs) believed noble warriors would be reborn as hummingbirds or butterflies after death, spending eternity in the House of the Sun, a flowery paradise in the East.

Where Songs Begin

1

Where can I gather the sweet-smelling flowers?
Whom should I ask? Should I pester the hummingbird,
Jade-bright and swift? Or bother the butterflies
That flit like the feathers of fiery gold birds?
They have the lore—they know the places
Where the sweet-smelling flowers bloom beautiful.

Alone I will wander the piney woods,
The peaks where the *tzinizcan* nests;
I will drift through the florid mangrove swamps
Where the roseate spoonbills wade and fish.
There they bend, heavy with glittering dew:
There they blossom beautiful. Maybe
I will find them there. Show them to me
And I will gather them up in my tilma—
With flowers I will greet the princes,
With flowers I will please the lords.

2

Yes, this place is where they live:
I hear their flowery song, echoed
By the mountains, call and response.
Ah, the water falls from springs in plumes,
Flowing blue like cotinga wings.
The mockingbird with four hundred songs
Sends forth her calls and answers herself.
The melodies of myriad songbirds thrum
With the rattle of the red-winged blackbird—
Hymns of praise to the Lord of Creation
That flood my soul and fill my throat.

3
With a mournful groan I call to them.
"O you whom He loves, ignore my intrusion."
They fall silent. A shimmering hummingbird asks,
"What are you looking for, Singer?"
"Where are some beautiful, sweet-smelling flowers
I can use to please your brothers-at-arms?"
A charm of the small birds chirps at me then:
"Follow us, Singer—we'll show you the way.
Perhaps with these blossoms you'll soon entertain
Those lordly warriors destined to join us."
4
I am led to a valley, land of plenty,
Land of flowers. They stretch before me,
Heavy with glittering dew—acres and
Acres of precious, sweet-smelling blooms,
Clothed in misty prisms of light.
The hummingbirds sing, "Cut all you want.
Enjoy yourself, Singer! When you return,
Give them to our lordly comrades
Whose deeds delight the Lord of Creation."
5
So I fill my tilma with fragrant flowers,
Pleasing the soul, spreading sweet bliss.
"I wish a friend had come with me:
Together we'd carry many more blooms.
But I know now the way. When I return,
I'll share the news with your comrades and mine—
We'll come here over and over, forever,
To gather the flowers, to learn every song,
And with them bring joy to our friends on earth:
Princely eagle and jaguar warriors."
6
I, the Singer, gather all that I can.
I flower-crown princes, put blooms in their hands.
From my lips the new songs slip:
I lift my voice in praise of those warriors
Before the Lord of the Near and the Nigh.

But what of those He deems unworthy?
Where do they go to gather such blossoms?
Could an unworthy soul, wretched and sinful,
Follow me east to the House of the Sun,
To that flowery land of plenty? Only
The Lord of the Near and the Nigh decides—
He makes us worthy or not of those songs.
And so my heart begins to weep.
I, the Singer, remember my walk
Through Paradise and cry out in despair:
7
"This earth is not a good place.
Joy lies elsewhere. What use is the earth?
True life exists where we're shorn of the flesh.
Let me go to that valley. Let my music mingle
With the song of those jade-bright birds.
Let me enjoy the precious flowers
That please the soul, that spread sweet joy,
Leaving me numb with delicious bliss."

(*Songs of Mexico*, I)

For the Nahuas, Tamoanchan was an ill-defined paradise from which the first humans emerged, often used synonymously with the 13-tiered heaven or with Tonatiuhchan, the House of the Sun, a paradise that awaits warriors killed in combat or sacrificed. Most Mesoamerican belief systems also referenced a world tree that serves as an axis mundi connecting the infernal, terrestrial and celestial planes (its roots enclosing the underworld and its branches supporting the heavens).

On Sacred Wings

1

The ancient Flower Tree is rooted fast
By the House of the Sun, where the precious maize blooms.
>From its branches come streaming the orioles, golden,
>The turquoise-browed motmots with blue racketed tails.
>Marvelous quetzals descend like feathered rainbows.

All of you birds will arrive from *Nonohualco*—
The Undying Shore—sent here by the Father,
For you are His creatures, His bright-plumed children.
>From those waters come streaming, you orioles golden
>And turquoise-browed motmots with blue racketed tails.
>Marvelous quetzals, descend like feathered rainbows.

2

That sacred maypole, festooned with jade-feather flowers,
Spreads its limbs across the turquoise House of Holy Writ.
In stillness it awaits the light of dawn.
>Your precious birds disturb Your sleep with cries,
>*Tzinizcans*, flamingos, blue cotingas:
>They grackle You awake, and then You dawn.

Their rattling voices harshly squawk and sing...
Rosy spoonbills, quetzals, golden orioles:
They grackle You awake, and then You dawn.

3

From *Tamoanchan*, where trees forever bloom,
From paradise arrive our greatest kings.
Moctezuma, Totoquihuaztli—
Here you stand in the courtyard of flowers,   [go to p. 16]

World Tree

Intoning the beautiful, ancient hymns.
You have come from the House of Holy Writ.
>It is as if you beat the flowered drums;
>It is as if you shook the rattle-blooms.
Intoning the beautiful, ancient hymns,
Here you stand in the courtyard of flowers.

4

From the place of His ash trees, of elders green,
The feathered god, that hummingbird, comes winging His way.
Leaving those bird-heavy boughs, how does He respond?
>He sucks up the honey we offer,
>Blissful—
>>As the flower opens its heart.

The holy butterfly flits back and forth,
Comes flying down, unfolding golden wings.
>He sucks up the honey we offer,
>Blissful—
>>As the flower opens its heart.

(*Songs of Mexico*, XXII)

Likely this poet's yearning was written by Aquiauhtzin, a nobleman and poet from the town of Ayapanco in the Chalco region, a tributary kingdom of the Aztec Triple Alliance.

The Poet's Yearning

Where do you dwell, my God,
Source and bane of my existence?
I seek you constantly,
A poet suffering in your absence,
      Yearning to delight you.

Fragrant white flowers—
Sweet words rain down
Like pale precious blooms
In the summer home of this your scribe,
      Yearning to delight you.

(*Songs of Mexico*, folio 10 r, lines 7-11)

The genre of verse called *tochcococuicatl* or rabbit-dove songs is purposefully bawdy, often written from the perspective of women (though the songs would have been performed by men dressed in female clothing). Despite the clear comic intent of the existing rabbit-dove or "wanton" dove songs, they contain the strong voices of women asserting their independence and viewing the world from unique perspectives.

Flower Mage

I arrive with the wind, twisting the greenery—
Holy Mother has made my heart giddy.
Could I ever hope to sleep?
I can already hear those beautiful melodies:
The songs of my flower mage.

Now the flower songs settle over us—
A turquoise moth, I playfully flit.
My heart is drunk on so many blossoms.
A precious tobacco bloom opens its petals:
In your hands I wander, my flower mage.
The blossoms spread...

Oh! I abandon myself to the dance...
Upon us fall such fragrant flowers!
I sing it once again, my love—
Oh! I abandon myself to the dance
Upon us fall such fragrant flowers!

Give up your flowers!
Give them up, my mage!
Popcorn flowers,
Cocoa blooms,
Oh!

Give up your flowers!
Give them up, my mage!
Popcorn flowers,
Cocoa blooms,
Oh! [go to p. 20]

Mage

Give!
Flower!
Give!
Cocoa bloom!
Give!

You!
My mage!
Come beat my drum!

(*Songs of Mexico*, LXXXVII-e)

For Nahua warriors, death in battle or in sacrifice to the sun was a glorious end that ensured one a place in the flowery paradise of Tonatiuhchan, the House of the Sun. There the warriors would accompany the rising sun each morning as it climbed to its zenith. Every four years they were said to descend to earth in the form of beautiful birds and butterflies, singing songs of praise to Tonatiuh or Huitzilopochtli, god of the sun.

Song of an Anxious Warrior

What choice? I crave it.
How else? Pursue it.
It's the divine flower.

O You through Whom Everything Lives:
By your will we common folk
Come to live upon the earth.
But how far will you spread
Your wealth of eagle flowers?

Ah, my heart pounds with fear—
Will I make it?

In moments I'll be on the battlefield,
Charging amidst the dust
From so many clanging shields.
They'll rain their arrows down
Like storms of deadly hail.

Ah, my heart pounds with fear—
Will I make it?

(*Songs of Mexico*, folio 25, lines 1-7)

This poem is attributed to Ayocuan, prince of Tecamachalco, a Chichimec kingdom conquered by the Aztec Triple Alliance in the late 15th century.

Evanescent Friendship

Let us enjoy ourselves, my friends,
Exchange warm embraces here and now.
For the moment we live on the flowered earth
Where no one can silence the eternal poem
That flows from the abode of the Giver of Life.

A fleeting moment on this earth...
It cannot be likewise in that Unknowable Realm.
Does happiness or friendship exist there Beyond?
No. Only here. The sole chance for connection is now.

(*Songs of Mexico*, folio 10 r, line 26 to folio 10 v, line 2)

This poem is another *tochcococuicatl* or rabbit-dove song.

Warm-blooded Woman

Ah, my heart is happy.
I'm a warm-blooded woman
Who finds herself at last
Among these older men
Far away from servant girls.

With my rainbow skirt,
O mother dear,
I hold myself tall and proud,
No nieces, girlfriends in my way—
I'm a precious flower,
And I'm everlasting!

Just like my mother did before,
I've come to rise above...
I'm a warm-blooded woman,
Far away from servant girls.

I've come to live a different life
Away from all the servant girls.
I'm a Huastec woman—
My popcorn buds are beautiful!

Forever here on earth?
Yes. Let me live like this:
Reviled by men or praised
As a wanton, lusty flower.

O my beating heart!
In the presence of the only God,
I hold myself tall and proud,
A woman on her own.

Jade stones are my rosary,
I gather them and count the beads.
My heart is full of joy--
I see those jades, my rosary:
I gather them and count the beads.

A gold-crowned parrot,
I am a prize.
Here I dwell,
An idle life...
I weep for you!

A goddess disguised as a doe,
I bound from my home
At the heart of paradise.

An honorable woman,
Crowned with this wreath
Of rainbow flowers,
I am *everyone's equal.*

A goddess disguised as a doe,
I bound from my home
At the heart of paradise.

(*Songs of Mexico*, LXXXVII-g)

"Matlatzinca Song" is attributed to Macuilxochitl, daughter of Tlacaelel, the man who rewrote history and religion, making the Mexica into the conquerors they are remembered as. This is the only existing poem composed by a Nahua woman in pre-Colombian times; it relates an incident involving Axaycatl, father of Moctezuma II, who assumed the throne at age 18 and died when he was 30, inspiring songwriters. The poet ironically uses a typical dance from Matlatzinco to praise the emperor for crushing a rebellion in that region.

Matlatzinca Song

I,   Macuilxochitl,
Strike up this tune
To gladden the Giver of Life:
Let the dancing begin!

Let this song be carried
To his dwelling place
In that Unknowable Realm.
Or do your flowers
Only blossom here?
Let the dancing begin!

Here's a Matlatzinca song,
A gift richly deserved,
Lord Itzcoatl:
Axayacatl, you tore down the city
Of Tlacotepec.
Your flowers and your butterflies
Went spiraling round Toluca
And Tlacotepec—
You gladdened our hearts
Like this Matlatzinca song.

> Gravely he offers
> Flowers and plumes
> To the Giver of Life.
> He lays eagle shields

In God's hands
In that dangerous place,
That burning plain:
The battlefield.

Like our songs, like our flowers,
You, too, shorn-headed prince,
Gladden the Giver of Life.

Eagle blooms rest
In both your hands,
Dear Axayacatl.
And He who stands
Forever at our side
Is burgeoning
With ocean flowers,
Fire buds—
Those blossoms of war—
Blissfully intoxicated.

The flowers of war
Blossom upon us
Here in Ehcatepec
In Mexico.
He who stands
Forever at our side
Is blissfully intoxicated.

The princes fought valiantly,
Acolhuans and Tepanecs.
Axayacatl cut a swath of conquests
Throughout Matlanzinco:
Malinalco, Ocuillan, Tecualoyan
And Xocotitlan.

He led his troops out
Through Xiquipilco,
And there Tlilat, an Otomi,
Wounded Axayacatl in the leg.

Once back in Mexico
The emperor spoke to his women,
Saying, "Prepare the loincloth,
The cape…all the prizes we award
Victorious warriors."
Then Axayacatl declared,
"Let the Otomi come forward
Who wounded me in the leg!"

Fear filled the Otomi.
"They will surely kill me," he thought.
So, in tribute, he brought thick timbers
And supple deerskins,
Bowing low before Axayacatl,
Sorely afraid.

But then Axayacatl's women
Gave him his just reward.

(Songs of Mexico, LXV)

Huitzilopochtli

The traditions of the Mexica tell how the god of war and of the sun, Huitzilopochtli, guided that tribe of Nahuas to Anahuac so they could construct a city there: Tenochtitlan, also known as Mexico, place of the Mexica. One of its most remembered rulers was Moctezuma II, who was warned by Nezahualpilli—liberal-minded ruler of Texcoco—that his hunger for control of the Triple Alliance would be its undoing. Angered, Moctezuma challenged the reformer to a ball game, which he lost. The emperor viewed this outcome as a chilling omen of Mexico's future.

The City of Huitzilopochtli

Spirals of jade encircle the city,
Mexico glitters quetzal-green.
Princes find rest in the shade of these walls—
A flowery mist spreads above them.

Behold your home, Giver of Life!
Here your word is law.
In Anahuac we hear your holy song—
It spreads above us all.

To this garden of white willows,
Of white rushes, delight of the Mexica,
You come winging down, a Great Blue Heron,
A god among his people.

Over the city you spread your wings,
You preen your turquoise plumes in Mexico,
While we your faithful vassals
Forever sing your worth.

Let none be captured walking here today.
Show us your mercy, Lord Moctezuma
And Totoquihuaztl, weaver of poems—
Kings who now accompany the sun.

Whom does the Giver of Life truly rule?
He has come to seize both heaven and earth.

Words of flame flare up, surging—
He sings them to the four winds.

Huitzilopochtli drapes this dawning light
In swaths about the city—
Tenochtitlan, where Moctezuma lost
To Nezahualpilli of Acolhuacan.

Already with His quetzal-feather fan
He shades us, sighing, moved.
How will Tenochtitlan prevail?
How will He sing those words now?

(*Songs of Mexico*, XXXV

This poem is attributed to Tecayehuatzin, a philosopher-poet who ruled in the Chichimec city-state of Huexotzinco. Like many Mexican kingdoms independent of Aztec rule, Huexotzinco took part in the Flower Wars (xochiyaoyotl) designed to provide sacrificial victims for the gods of each city-state.

Holy Dance

Flowers have been scattered:
Let the dance begin, my friends,
Yonder by the beating drums.
All of them await His presence—
Anguish rules our hearts.

Hark! He comes...Creation's Lord...
Dropping down from heaven's bourn,
Singing as he nears—
Round about, the unseen conches
Echo every note.

(*Songs of Mexico*, folio 10 v, lines 24-28)

Totoquihuaztl was a ruler of Tlacopan, one of the three city-states in the Aztec Triple Alliance.

Let the Singer Come

Why then should I begin in vain
My song before the Lord of Life?
My wretched verse is poor indeed!

Let the singer come and gladden you true,
O Giver of Life, with turquoise wisdom,
Bright songs he has forged and drilled,
To string like holy beads.

As for me, I am utterly wretched. What grief!
I would gladden you, but my skill is weak.
A middling singer, an orphan bereft,
I sigh my plight before you.

These poor flowers, my humble songs,
I croon to you, my only Lord,
By whose will the universe moves.

There where you live you are flooded with joy,
O Giver of Life: throughout the cosmos
You are worshipped with music.

These poor flowers, my humble songs,
I croon to you, my only Lord,
By whose will the universe moves.

Yes, I sing, and my flowers spread,
My song spreads toward you.
I drill the jade, I smelt the gold—
     This is my song.
I mount the emeralds in the air—
     They are my song.

A wretch, but I can gladden you.
I call him. Let the singer come.
I am Totoquihuaztl, poet-prince—
        Surely he can bring you joy.
Let the singer come through me
        And he will free your songs.

Such a fortunate man to have such songs,
To polish them like emeralds,
To whirl them in gorgeous circles.

Let the singer come—
Totoquihuaztl.
Let him come.

        A *tzinizcan*, a swan, a blue cotinga:
        Such are your guises, Giver of Life,
        As you sip from the painted flowers,
        Many-hued songs inscribed in our hearts.

        You open wide your quetzal wings,
        You stir the air with *tzinizcan* plumes,
        Holy indigo swan.

        Come sip here, delighted,
        From the fragrant blooms
        That slowly drift to earth.

(*Songs of Mexico*, XXXV)

During the latter part of the 14th and beginning of the 15th centuries, the independent Nahua confederacy of Chalco became a tributary of the Aztec Triple Alliance, participating in elaborate flower wars (xochiyaoyotl) with the empire designed to provide sacrificial victims for each side. Real war erupted in 1446 when Chalco refused to contribute materials for the construction of a temple to Huitzilopochtli. After two decades of conflict, the Triple Alliance defeated Chalco. When the Spaniards arrived in Mexico a half century later, Chalco quickly allied with the conquistadores to bring about the downfall of the empire they viewed as oppressors.

During the War with Chalco

Let eagle and jaguar warriors
Begin to embrace, you princes.
The shields are rattling, rattling—
Captives are bartered with blood.

Upon our heads they scatter,
Upon us rain those battle flowers,
The One God's greatest joy.
The shields are rattling, rattling—
Captives are bartered with blood.

Seething there upon the field
The fire stirs and surges.
Honor is won, shields bring fame,
As dusty chime our ankle bells.

Never will the war blooms tire—
They gather at the river's edge.
Jaguar buds and shield flowers:
They open wide their petals,
As dusty chime our ankle bells.

Jaguar cocoa blossoms
Are shaken down and spread
Across the battlefield.
Oh, which of you truly wants it?
There pride and honor await.

Discordant flowers bring no joy.
But heart blooms are grown
Upon the field, beside the war—
Princes depart, they rise...
There pride and honor await.

With cane eagle shields,
Jaguar banners are joined.
With quetzal-feather shields.
Plumed pennants are arrayed—
Foaming, they twist in the wind.
Chalcans and Amaquemes flee.
War is fanned to a crackling hiss.

The mighty spears are shivered,
Shattered their tips of obsidian—
Shield dust settles over us.
Chalcans and Amaquemes flee.
War is fanned to a crackling hiss.

(*Songs of Mexico*, XXIV)

The Mexica of Tenochtitlan were the most powerful of the Aztec Triple Alliance, an empire shared among the Tepanecs, the Acolhuans and the Mexica. The historical figures mentioned in this poem date from the early years of the alliance, whose army had several orders or societies, including the eagle and jaguar warriors. Note that Acolmiztli is the second name of the revered Acolhuan poet Nezahualcoyotl.

Undefeated

Sprouting, greenly blossoming,
Are the tears and the words
Of Acolmiztli and his grandsire
Techotlala, lords of Acolhuacan;
Of Acamapichtli, first Mexica king
There where the prickly pear stands;
And of Tezozomoc, long-lived lord
Of the Dry Lands, Tepanecapan.
Their legacy, their command, lives on.

On the mats of eagle warriors
And among the jaguar knights
A prayer goes up to the Divine Mother.
And the Master of Life,
Who was born on his shield,
Drops black as night
Over Mexico.

White chalk and feathers rain down,
Landing here on this earth.
Your duty, your wealth, O Princes
Cuatlecoatl and Cahualtzin,
Borrowed bits of the glory of God,
Who was born on his shield,
Who drops black as night
Over Mexico.

The fame of Tenochtitlan has spread,
The city is honored throughout the land.
No one fears that sacred death,
O princes. God commands it of you.
Thus good things are given.

Who could truly set His shield to rest?
His throne? His mighty spear?
Think on that. Remember it well, O princes.
Who could lay waste to Tenochtitlan?
Who dares assail the foundation of heaven?

May Mexico forever endure!
May the Master of Life
Keep us hidden in peace.
For as long as He brightens the skies
We will always exist.

(*Songs of Mexico*, XXVII)

The Aztec army boasted many different elite military orders, most restricted to men of noble birth. But two of the most prestigious warrior societies, the eagle and jaguar knights, prided themselves on recruiting the very bravest fighters alive. As a result, many commoner infantrymen, after daring deeds on the battlefield, were permitted to join the orders.

Three Kings and the Warrior Societies

O Moctezuma, O Nezahualcoyotl, O Totoquihuaztl—
You whirled and you spun nobility's code.
At least for a moment take hold of your cities,
Where once you were glorious kings!

Where the eagles perch, where the jaguars crouch,
City of cities, standing forever—Mexico!
Many-hued beautiful flowers of war
Loosen their battle cries, striving together,
Shaken and yearning for your return.

Eagles transform into men on that field;
Jaguars snarl commands there in Mexico.
There you govern still, Moctezuma!
Dancers there celebrate valiant deeds,
Eagle society woven with Jaguar knights—
Their might is made known on the plain.

With flowery eagle cords the city is moored,
As jaguar blossoms the kings have been braided—
Moctezuma, Cahualtzin, Totoquihuaztl,
The poet we name Yoyontzin.
In our arrows and our battle shields
This city of cities continues to stand.

(Songs of Mexico, XXIX)

The Vanity of Song

Though the labor be in vain, my friends,
Take pleasure in our song, our song.
Pick up your precious drums and beat!
Shake loose the flowers, spread them well—
      Even if they finally wilt!

We'll also lift our newborn songs,
The freshest blooms here in our hands—
Find joy in them, our dearest friends,
They'll soothe the pain of bitter lives.

Let none be sad or ponder the world—
Behold our flowers and beautiful songs!
Find joy in them, our dearest friends,
They'll soothe the pain of bitter lives.

It's only here on earth, my friends,
We're lent to each other, for at the end
We leave the beautiful songs behind...
We leave the beautiful blooms behind.

Though it's your tune, it saddens me,
Composer of our fleeting lives—
We leave the beautiful songs behind...
We leave the beautiful blooms behind.

                  (*Songs of Mexico,* folio 33 v, lines 6-18)

Younger brother of Moctezuma II, Tlacahuepan was a *tlacochcalcatl* or high general of the Aztec army who died during a flower war with Huexotzinco, becoming a symbol of heroism in battle.

Upon the Death of Tlacahuepan

A clamor of bells
Out on the plains.
There, forsaken,
Lies Tlacahuepan.

With yellowed flowers
He sweetly reeks
Toward the vast
Unknowable Realm.

In Chicomoztoc
You hide, Place
Of Seven Caves,
Land of mesquite.

The eagle cries,
The jaguar roars,
And you, fire-red swan,
Wheel through the skies—

Leaving the plains
For the Unknowable Realm.

(*Songs of Mexico,* folio 22 r, lines 27-31)

Tamoanchan Symbol

Though Huitzilopochtli, god of war and the sun, was the focus of much Aztec religious activity, their principal deity was Tezcatlipoca, a creator god associated with jaguars, magic, darkness, rulership, strife and violence. Tezcatlipoca was feared and reverenced, and the Nahuas had many names for him, including Titlacahuan (We Are His Slaves), Ipalnemoani (Giver of Life), Necoc Yaotl (Enemy on Both Sides), Tloque Nahuaque (Lord of the Near and the Nigh) and Moquequeloa (The Mocker). Much of the verse in compiled in Songs of Mexico and Ballads of the Lords of New Spain was likely originally addressed to him, though the Conquest required a retrofitting so that Tezcatlipoca became, essentially, Yahweh/Jehovah.

Conquered Cities

The Giver of Life makes us suffer, my princes!
With a word he simply commands:
Perhaps where the rushes grow thick like capes,
Or high upon cliffs that loom over rivers?
Right here, in Chalco.

Your fame will never fade away,
You whose title is Giver of Life.
Here where the bells lie broken,
Battle blossoms and shield blooms.
Where the chalk and the feathers are scattered,
The paper plumes all strewn about.
Where heart flowers spread their petals wide—
Right here, in Chalco.

Abandoned and desolate stands
Itztompatepec, obsidian heights.
Nevermore that former glory,
Nevermore those joyous songs:
Your heart will feel pity when it finally cools,
Mocker of Men, Giver of Life.
You torment your princes,
The sobbing of your subjects rises.

Let us not be frightened by war:
Those are only shield blooms, you princes—
Only through such can we name and record
The Fathers and Mothers who stood here before.
The earth will return to a peaceful state.
Your heart will feel pity when it finally cools.

Consider this and weep, you princes
Of Chalco and Amaquemecan—
Upon our roofs the shields are lifted
Against the arrows thick as mist.

What has the Giver of Life decreed?
The city of Chalco is eaten by flame!
His subjects are fleeing in every direction!
Let that be enough! Let this judgment be ended!
Let the Giver of Life feel pity at last!

In the place of the bells, where battle is waged,
The reeds all lie broken in Chalco today.
Dust yellows the air, our houses are smoking,
The sobbing is rising—from the lips of your Chalcans!

Never undone, never forgotten,
That which the One God has wrought—
Felled and scattered forever, Itztompatepec:
Dust yellows the air, our houses are smoking,
The sobbing is rising—from the lips of your Chalcans!

You rule from your cities, King Moctezuma
And Prince Nezahualcoyotl:
You ravage the land, and you devastate Chalco—
Let your hearts feel pity at last!

As you whirl your festive dance across the earth,
You ravage the land, and you devastate Chalco—
Let your hearts feel pity at last!

(Songs of Mexico, LI-b)

A Poet's Wealth

I am choosing all your greatest songs,
Assembling emeralds, gathering bracelets
That dangle golden prawns.
Adorn yourself with pride—
These flowers are your riches.

In a burst of gorgeous plumes,
Up fly your *tzinizcans*, your fire-red swans.
You use those feathers
To trim your drum on the earth—
These flowers are your riches.

(*Songs of Mexico,* folio 34 v, lines 2-6)

Monkey Scribes

44

Nahua priests taught of thirteen spheres or "heavens" above our earth and of nine levels of the underworld beneath this plane. The highest divinity was named Ometeotl, "the god of duality," and it inhabited the thirteenth heaven: Omeyocan, "the place of duality," the cosmic origin of all things. Ometeotl embraced both halves of dualities: both the feminine and the masculine, as well as other complementary pairs (light-dark, positive-negative, spirit-matter). All Nahua gods can be seen as facets or emanations of Ometeotl. The idea of duality as the source of existence predates the rise of the Mexica: it is depicted in a frieze at Teotihuacan, the Toltec temple located northeast of Mexico City, which shows Ometeotl creating the universe out of itself. The Nahua believed that upon death, most people were destined to Mictlan, the underworld, where they would face a four-year journey of trials before finding their eternal rest. Mictlan was also known as Ximoayan, Place of the Shorn (or of the Bodiless).

Uncertainty

Where will I go?
Oh, where will I go?
God stands double yet one.
Difficult. Difficult.

They say that future home lies
In the Place of the Shorn—
Our bodiless souls—
Deep in heaven's heart.

But what if it is only *here*?
Could the Place of the Shorn
Be right here on this earth?

We are forever pilgrims,
We leave to never return—
No one remains on this earth.

Those who would ask
Where our friends are—
Be glad.

                (*Songs of Mexico,* folio 35 v, line 27 to folio 36 r, line 2)

Huexotzinco was Chichimec-related city-state whose inhabitants also claimed relation to the Acolhua of Coatlinchan. Huexotzinco boasted a circular temple dedicated to Ehecatl, the wind god, a manifestation of Quetzalcoatl, the principal adversary of Tezcatlipoca, main deity of the Aztec Triple Alliance. The patron of Huexotzinco, however, was the hunting god, Mixcoatl Camaxtli. This city state was one of the few to defeat the Triple Alliance: in 1506, they brought Tenochtitlan to its knees and captured thousands of Aztec warriors. They later helped the Spaniards seal the Aztecs' doom.

Siege of Huexotzinco

Envied and hated,
The city of Huexotzinco,
Like some blockaded cactus,
Bristles thick with spears.
Turtle-shell timpani thrum
In your houses, Huexotzinco—
There Tecayehuatzin stands guard,
There Lord Quecehuatl chants
        And plays his flute,
        Alone in his chambers.

Ah, listen closely, all:
Our father has descended.
In Jaguar house the pounding drums—
Timpani songs come rolling out.

His quetzal cape stretches forth
Like blossoms toward the sun—
Guarded in the House of Holy Writ,
Where city and land and god are kept.

Flaming, flowery arrows fall
Upon your jade-green home.
This golden house of written words—
Your dwelling place, my God.

                (*Songs of Mexico,* folio 12 v, line 9-21)

This humorous poem features a priest from Calpan, a small pueblo associated with Huexotzinco (and therefore an enemy of the Triple Alliance). The poem can be read as both a ribald satire of Calpan morality as well as a critique of Nahuas who abandon their faith to follow the teachings of Catholic priests.

Tempted by a Priest

A Calpan priest keeps coming round
And sits in the plaza, crying out,
"Sweet kid! Ah, you scaredy-cat…
Dear flower! You garland, you!"

I ignore him. He keeps it up:
"Hey, little brother! Nephew!
Beloved boy! Nephew!
Most handsome of them all!
Nephew, come over to the plaza!
I brought you some roasted cherry pits…
Here! Hey! You should greet me
With a 'dear priest,' my boy."

Some secretly listen to his "Hey! Hey!"
Who are the ones who wander close,
Having believed his tender words after all?
The guys we love, our old companions.

"My little brother, you're angry, no?
Your hands are red from scrubbing…
You're all fed up, I'll bet.
Forever on earth? Pshaw, my young page.
Hey. Little lord. Come *here*.
Don't be sad. Don't let your voice creak
As if you were sick, citizen.

"Life Giver God will cleanse the world.
Meanwhile, laugh! Tickle your tool a bit
Here in this paradise.

Soon enough we'll pass away.
We'll perish once and for all.

"Last night I got pretentiously drunk,
Gorgeously drunk. And I'm drunk again,
Boy. I'm betting your heart feels it, no?
Take my hand. Let's head home already.

"He just drank it...
Yes! He drank it!
Oh, naughty little boy
Let's go!
He drank it!"

(*Songs of Mexico,* LXXXVIII)

Poems from
Ballads of the Lords of New Spain

This poem is attributed to Tecayehuatzin, a philosopher-poet who ruled in the Chichimec city-state of Huexotzinco. Tlaxcala was another Chichimec city-state. Both participated in flower wars with the Triple Alliance.

Showers of Songs for the Bards

Let us sing, my friends!
Let us join and share songs
In the flowery heat that flows
From the House of the Sun.
But who will find them?
Where does one look?
And how is the search begun,
Here beside the drums?

I grieve for those flowers,
I, your sad friend,
The Chichimec lord
Tecayehuatzin.
But who among us
Will no longer gladden,
Hopes no longer to please
The Self-Made God?

Oh, there in that distant Tlaxcala,
That handsome city, they intone
My flowery, lethargic songs.
May those drowsy tunes be sung
By the greatest bards:
Xicotencatl, Temilotzin and
Prince Cuitlizcatl!
Let divine words ring: *ohuaya!*

Huexotzinco is Heaven,
The Tamoanchan of Eagle Lords,
The House of Jaguar Darkness.
Behold the field where the Dancer died—
Our dear Tlacahuepan.

Right there in his House of Spring
His garlanded sons, his noble princes,
Each finds true contentment.
With cocoa flowers they come,
Dancing as they shout for joy
Delighting in flowers there
At the water's edge.
They arrive brandishing
Their golden shields,
Their feathered fans,
With headdresses of war-red plumes.
"With flags of quetzal feathers
We are here to gladden hearts
Within the House of Spring!"

The jade-encrusted cymbals crash,
A fragrant rain of blossoms
Showers down upon the earth,
Upon the black-feathered palace
At the heart of the battlefield.
Her son is now descending!
In spring he drops down from on high:
The Giver of Life!
His songs wrap round like husks of maize,
He festoons himself with flowers here
Beside the beating drum.
Such intoxicating blooms!
They are twisted into garlands
As they swirl from your souls...
Drown yourselves in ecstasy!

(*Ballads of the Lords of New Spain,* I)

The title Moyocoyatzin (Self-maker) was given both to Tezcatlipoca, the capricious supreme deity of the Aztecs, and to Ometeotl, the divine duality. The former is clearly intended in the following song of praise.

Praising the Self-Made God

The dwelling of the Self-Made God
Is in no single place—
Everywhere He's called upon,
Everywhere He's praised
By those on earth who seek to spread
His glory and His fame.

He crafts His songs with holy words
Unknown to man: *ohuaya!*
Everywhere He's called upon,
Everywhere He's praised
By those on earth who seek to spread
IIis glory and His fame.

No human being, no living man,
Can be Life Giver's friend.
Only when we praise his name,
Only in his presence,
Only by his side,
Can life exist on earth.

Whoever finds the Self-Made God
Finds comfort and joy.
Only when we praise his name,
Only in his presence,
Only by his side,
Can life exist on earth.

> No one is ever truly your friend,
> O Lord of All That Lives:
> You see us as nothing but flowers,
> Heaped high upon the earth,

There by your side.
Soon your heart will tire of us—
Just the briefest of moments
There with you, by your side.

He makes our hearts grow mad,
Life Giver does,
He makes us drunk.
No one could hope to escape
From the ruler of earth.

We simply annoy him,
However much our hearts cry out.
No one could hope to escape
From the ruler of earth.

(Ballads of the Lords of New Spain, IV)

Atl tlachinolli

This is Cacamatzin, last king of Texcoco, remembering during a trying time the power and greatness of his father and grandfather. Cacamatzin was captured, tortured and killed by the Spanish in 1520.

The King of Texcoco Remembers

Friends, listen to what I just heard:
"Let no one go marching off to war
Like some ancient lord.
Let anger and quarreling
Fall into oblivion and perish
From the face of this good earth!"

Even me, their king!
They even criticize *me*.
At the ball court,
During the sacrifice,
They were simpering, saying,
"How can this be human?
  How can he be sane?"

Who knows what else
They babble about...
But is it not true
That I rule on this earth?

Smoke curls from the guns.
Let the horns sound the call.
Upon my head, upon the earth
The blossoms begin to fall,
Twisting and whirling,
Bringing their pleasures to earth.

This is how it must be
In the House of the Sun,
How it must forever be
In that far green land,
The Giver of Life painting the world
With gorgeous tobacco blooms.

Where the jade-fretted log drums are sounding,
Where the jade flutes are being played,
That is the love of the owner of heaven,
Scarlet feathers that bend to the ground,
Heavy with dewdrop jewels divine.

A song-shield mist, a shower of darts:
The heavens are howling
With flowers and darkness.
The dance is begun
With shields of gold.

Here I am, Cacama,
The only one speaking—
I imagine my father,
King Nezahualpilli...
Is he seen, is he advised
By Nezahualcoyotl,
His venerable sire,
There by the drums?
I remember them still...

Who will not go there?
Whether jade or gold,
Who will not truly go?
Am I perhaps
A turquoise shield,
Shattered,
Waiting for repair?

I shall go forth to battle,
Wrapped up in my finest cape—
And here, on earth,
Beside those pounding drums,
I will remember them!

(*Ballads of the Lords of New Spain,* V)

Tlaltecatl (also known by his honorific Tlaltecatzin) was the first king of Texcoco, an Acolhuan city-state that under his rule became a center of culture and wisdom. This is his only known poem.

Ode to Fleeting Love

I come to guard the city
Where I am praised.
Using his flowers as paint,
The Giver of Life
Creates brotherhood.

But you have been left
Alone in your mansion,
O Tlaltecatl.
You sigh,
You whisper.

Together with my god
You sing,
You sigh,
You whisper.

> Fire-red bird,
> You are flaring up,
> Your flowery diadem
> Sets me aflame.
> You, mother,
> Sweet-smelling woman,
> Blazing popcorn bloom,
> You are only borrowed:
> You will be abandoned,
> And then you, too, will leave.
> All will be shorn of the flesh.

You have arrived
Among the princes,
You lovely creature.
There you perch, my blue cotinga,
Standing on my feathered mat,
Blazing popcorn bloom,
You are only borrowed:
You will be abandoned,
And then you, too, will leave.
All will be shorn of the flesh.

The flowering cocoa plant
Flickers with flame,
The tobacco bloom is offered up:
If my heart takes her in,
She will make my heart drunk.

But no more will she be here
On the earth, my princes!
If my heart takes her in,
She will make my heart drunk.

And so I just grieve, groaning,
"Let me not go
To the Place of the Shorn:
My heart is now precious...
For I, I am a poet—
And my flower is golden."

But I leave her behind.
I see my new home,
Surrounded by blooms.
Will great emeralds
And broad quetzal plumes
Be my reward?

I surrender myself to you,
My Lord; I say,
"Let me pass away!

Let me be bundled and burned,
Poet though I be!
Let it happen this way!
Let not my heart be her captive!"

Thus will I simply leave,
My heart accompanied by flowers
And spinning quetzal feathers,
Transformed into precious jade
Whose like is not found on the earth.

Let it happen...
But peacefully.

(*Ballads of the Lords of New Spain,* VI)

During the first decade of the 16th century, the Triple Alliance engaged in series of flower wars with the nations of Atlixco and Huexotzinco. Toward the end, the younger brother of Moctezuma II, Tlacahuepan, led the Aztec army on the battlefield. The tide of war began to turn against the Aztecs, depressing their morale. The general, with a ferocious glee that would become legendary, hurled himself against the enemy forces to inspire his own men. After slaughtering dozens of Huexotzincans, he allowed himself to be captured as a sacrificial victim. He demanded the enemy kill him on the battlefield, however, among the corpses of his victims. They tore his body to pieces, and the prince became a symbol of the perfect warrior.

Moctezuma Mourns His Brother's Death

War smoke and shield clash rise
O Yaotzin, Our Enemy, fierce Lord of the Bells—
Smoke and clash are your flowers, O God.
Yonder the mass of eagles and jaguars
Howl their battle cry.

For a moment He becomes our friend,
Has mercy on our captain.
That flower of flesh has ripened:
It drops to the ground
As black blades slash,
Attaining greatness.

Battle-slain, our captain rises
To the flowery land beside the water,
House of the butterflies
That shield the sun.
No longer with the darts of war
Or precious flower spears
Can we compare our prince:
Moctezuma's painted book,
Nevermore in Mexico—
He has gone away and left
The flower of the flesh behind.   [go to p. 62]

Moctezuma II Signature Glyph

The flowers all are blossoming:
High above, his song begins.
No longer with the darts of war
Or precious flower spears
Can we compare our prince:
Moctezuma's painted book,
Nevermore in Mexico—
He has gone away and left
The flower of the flesh behind.

Your fire-red bird resplendent flies,
You leave this world, Prince Tlacahuepan.
And as you glimmer with rainbow light,
God comes to shear your flesh away.

Above us, there Beyond,
The blaze roils and rages and roars,
Burning all,
Until golden flowers shower down.
And there you remain,
My dear prince,
My brother,
Tlacahuepan.

Oh! I grieve,
My heart aches with sadness
I see him yonder,
Bereft as an orphan,
Like feathers carelessly shaken
Onto the ground.

I go to where victorious warriors
Array themselves with flowers,
But still I see him yonder,
Bereft as an orphan,
Like feathers carelessly shaken
Onto the ground.

(*Ballads of the Lords of New Spain*, XXVII)

This poem is attributed to Nezahualcoyotl, a poet-king of Texcoco under whom the arts flourished. A gloss in the manuscript claims the song was written when the poet was fleeing from the king of Azcapotzalco, whose men drove Nezahualcoyotl into exile.

Nezahualcoyotl's Song of Flight

I vain was I born.
I vain I emerged
From the House of the Sun
To walk this bitter earth
And live a wretched life.

Truly I should not have emerged.
Better I had never been born.
An easy avowal. Yet...what shall I do,
O princes who have also descended?
Must I live in the public eye?
No other way...One must be prudent.

Must I drag myself erect
All alone upon the earth?
Is this emptiness all that I merit?
I feel nothing but absolute misery.
My heart aches, my absent friends,
Faced with the impossible task
          Of living with my fellow man.

How does one live among others?
Does a cruel, rude existence
Give people a sense of power?
Just live calmly, in simple peace!
All I can do is show obeisance,
Bow my head before the others.

So I weep from the depths of despair,
Alone—forsaken—amidst the human throng.
How has Your heart elected this fate,

O You through Whom Everything Lives?
Let Your anger wane, Your compassion spread:
I yearn to be at Your side, my God...
   ...or are you perhaps preparing my death?

Could we ever be truly happy
To merely live upon this earth?
Ah, we certainly exist,
And we were sent here to find joy.
Yet every single one of us
Succumbs at last to misery:
      Bitterness and anguish rule
      In each human's mind.

Do not despair, my heart.
Stop your fruitless contemplation.
There is little compassion
To be had in this world.
Even when I feel *You* by my side,
O You through Whom Everything Lives,
      Bitterness spreads like poison.

I can only search for, remember
The friends I have lost.
Will they return again?
No, a single time do we vanish,
Just once from here on the earth.
But let not their hearts be heavy,
      There by His side, eternally with Him,
      He through Whom Everything Lives.

(*Ballads of the Lords of New Spain*, XIX)

The Answer to Doubt

"Do you exist?
Do you really exist?"
Asks some drunk
Who has come to rave.

"The Giver of Life...
Is he real? Is he false?"
How could anyone
Possibly ask that?

Let not our hearts be troubled! Oh!

So much that is true
They claim is false.
But the Giver of Life
Is simply capricious.

Let not our hearts be troubled! Oh!

O Lord, Giver of Life,
I was greatly distressed—
Who isn't sometimes
Distressed by those doubts?
I was never content
Among my fellows.

But you lovingly shake them out,
Riches drop from your hands,
Giver of Life—
Popcorn flowers,
Cocoa blooms.

Oh, how I longed for them!
I was greatly distressed.

(*Ballads of the Lords of New Spain*, XVIII)

God's Paintings

With blossoms you paint us,
Giver of Life,
With songs you color everything
That ever will exist,
Hatching eagle society
And jaguar warriors.
Only through your art
Do we live on this earth.

And thus you sketch the contours
Of friendship, brotherhood, nobility.
With songs you color everything
That ever will exist,
Hatching eagle society
And jaguar warriors.
Only through your art
Do we live on this earth.

Let the nobles sit on thrones
Or hide in cages of jade:
We each stand alone.
We each deserve our deaths,
Every last human being.
All of us will leave the earth—
All of us will die.

I perceive His secret, His cage,
O noble peers of mine!
We each stand alone.
We each deserve our deaths,
Every last human being.
All of us will leave the earth—
All of us will die.

None becomes jade,
None becomes gold,
Installed here on earth.
All of us will leave
To that Unknown Realm.
None will remain,
All will be consumed—
We are headed for His home.

Like paintings
We fade away,
Like flowers
We wither on earth.
Like feathers
Of quetzals, orioles,
Jade-green motmots
We will be consumed at last.
We are headed for His home.

Our God has arrived,
Enveloped in sadness,
Living within it.
Not in vain are those eagles
And jaguars mourned...
We will be consumed at last.
None will remain.

Ponder it, my noble peers,
Eagles and jaguars all—
Were you jade,
Were you gold,
You would go just the same
To the Place of the Shorn.
We will be consumed at last.
None will remain.

(Ballads of the Lords of New Spain, XXIX)

The Path to Glory

Emeralds, gold
Are your flowers
My Lord!

Such are your riches,
Giver of Life:
Death by black blade,
Or wartime demise.

Through battle death
You win eternal fame,
My brothers.

Amid flinty war,
At the edge
Of conflagration,
You will be known.

The dust of shields
Is spreading wide;
Broadly roils
The smoke of spears.

Do you truly believe
You could ever find fame
In that Unknowable Realm?

To win glory, renown—
You must die on the battlefield.
Thus you draw nigh
To the Place of the Shorn.

(*Ballads of the Lords of New Spain*, XXX)

This song is attributed to Nezahualcoyotl. The piece is a *xopancuicatl*—
"green" or "spring" song.

A Song of Spring

In the House of Holy Writ
God composes songs,
Experimenting
With sound.
> He scatters flowers,
> Delights us with music.

His songs jingle:
Ankle bells approach.
Our flower rattles
Respond.
> He scatters flowers,
> Delights us with music.

The sweet *chachalaca*
Croons over these blooms,
Unfolding its music
Upon the water.

A bevy of swans
Trumpet in answer
To the beautiful bird
That truly sings.

Your heart, my Lord,
Is a book of songs.
You stand here singing
And beating your drum.
> You are the singer:
> Amidst the greening of spring
> You bring joy to your children.

You scatter drowsy blooms
And cocoa blossoms.
> You are the singer:
> Amidst the greening of spring
> You bring joy to your children.

You offer us blossoms,
Millions of blooms,
Bringing joy to your brethren,
Prince Nezahualcoyotl.
> My heart understands:
> In your hands they endure
> For you twist out a garland
> Of springtide flowers.

From the Place of Duality,
From Heaven they whirl
Bringing joy to all people,
Prince Nezahualcoyotl.
> My heart understands:
> In your hands they endure
> For you twist out a garland
> Of springtide flowers.

Cuatlecoatl was the son of Acamapichtli, first ruler of Tenochtitlan. He served as a teuctlahtoh or judge during the reign of his half-brother Huitzilihuitl and was later given the rank of tlacochcalcatl or commanding general. His nephews were Moctezuma I and Tlacaelel, who would later transform the city-state into one of the most powerful kingdoms in Mesoamerica. Cuatlecoatl died in battle.

Princely Duty

Princes never waste the day
While they carry their shields
At the ready.

Let him not be afflicted or sad.
War is riches,
War is joy.

General Cuatlecoatl,
Long departed,
Knows God.

(Ballads of the Lords of New Spain, XXXV)

"Chalk and feathers" is a Nahuatl kenning for "sacrificial victims" or "ritual death." Aztec warriors who died were bundled tightly in funeral shrouds and cremated with birds and butterflies, symbols of their transformation into the companions of the sun.

A Warrior's End

Like emeralds,
Turquoise—
Your chalky clay and white funereal feathers,
O He Who Lets Us Live.

Your princes
Are blissful now:
Freed in flowery death by obsidian blade
Or battle-slain, bundled, burned.

(*Ballads of the Lords of New Spain*, XXXVI)

Death Bundle

Other Selected Nahuatl Poetry

Attributed to Nezahualcoyotl, this poem appears in Spanish on the Mexican 100-peso note.

Brotherhood

I love the song of the mockingbird,
bird of four hundred voices;
I love the color of jade and the drowsy perfume
of the flowers;
but more than these, I love
my fellow man.

I have taken a few liberties in crafting an English version of this song, from Franciscan missionary Bernardino de Sahagún's *First Memoranda*, in order to more clearly show how Teteoinnan, mother of the gods, assumes the form of other goddesses. Note the reference to her legendary encounter with two Chichimec heroes toward the end.

Hymn for the Divine Mother

The golden flower starts to bloom:
Our mother slips from paradise—
Tamoanchan, the birthplace of the gods—
Her holy face so pale, so smooth.

Golden petals slowly open,
From heaven She emerges now:
Heart of the earth, Teteoinnan, goddess ,
Her lips are painted black as night.

The salt-white flower starts to bloom:
Our mother slips from paradise—
Tamoanchan, the birthplace of the gods—
Red circles on Her holy face.

Chalky petals slowly open,
From heaven She emerges now:
Our grandmother Toci, healer and midwife,
Her lips are painted black as night.

The goddess alights on a barrel cactus,
In the guise of Itzpapalotl,
Black-taloned butterfly.

You have seen Her cross the nine bleak deserts:
Deer hearts sated Her hunger,
Our mother Tlaltecuhtli.

Alas, the funereal chalk is fresh;
She is newly clad in pure white plumes;
On every side the arrows lie.

But death is just illusion—
You transform into a deer
And the hunter-heroes Xiuhnel and Mimich
Show You mercy in the wild.

This poem is from *Codex Matritense*, and is attributed to the Teotihuacans.

Death Rite

It is like they used to say:
In the end, we die,
But it is not truly death.
We live, we rouse ourselves,
We continue to exist, we leave this place.
But some hesitate
Before flying to Him;
Therefore, at the end,
When people die,
We speak to them.

If a man has passed away,
We say, speaking to him
As we would a god,
"Cuecuextzin,
O Jeweled Armband!"
If a woman has died,
We say, "Chamotzin,
O Dark Red Feather!

"Take flight! Depart!
The light of dawn
Has tinged the sky
A crimson hue!
Scarlet parrots are singing
With ruddy barn swallows—
Scarlet butterflies flit about,
Very much alive."

This they said,
The ancient ones:
"Anyone who dies
Turns to dust."

Thus they spoke:
"All who die
Turn to dust—
But that is not the end."

Cihuateotl

In Aztec tradition, the souls of women who died giving birth are transformed into fierce, fighting spirits known as cihuapipiltin (princesses), mocihuaquetzque (those who arise as women) or, most commonly, cihuateteo (deified women). The Aztecs honored them in the same way they would warriors killed in battle, and it was believed that they could be called on to give soldiers more strength and bravery on the battlefield. The ancients also claimed that the cihuateteo emerged from their paradise in the West every evening to accompany the sun as it slid down the western sky to the Underworld. It was important to revere a cihuateotl correctly, as they were known to haunt crossroads and steal children if ritual was neglected.

To a Woman Who Has Died during Childbirth

Chamotzin, my youngest child,
Cuauhcihuatl, little one,
Sweet dove, my beloved daughter:
You have toiled, you have labored,
And now your work is at an end.

You aided your Mother,
The goddess Cihuacoatl,
The Lady Quilaztli.
You seized and lifted
And wielded the shield,
The holy buckler set in your hands
By your Mother,
The goddess Cihuacoatl,
The Lady Quilaztli.

Now waken and rise—
A new day is dawning.
The sun's crimson feathers are filling the sky.
Scarlet parrots and swallows warble their calls.
Wedges of fire-bright swans sing along.

So waken and rise! Make yourself beautiful!
Come! Learn of the good place, that sweet land,
The home of your Mother and Father, the Sun.

There you'll be joyful, content,
Pleasured, prosperous.

Come! Follow our Mother and Father, the Sun.
Let his elder sisters fly you to him,
Those warrior princesses, celestial women,
Who always and forever know joy,
Contentment, pleasure, prosperity
There beside our Mother and Father, the Sun,
Bringing Him joy with their shouts of praise.

My youngest child, my beloved daughter,
My Lady—
You have worn yourself out,
You have fought like a warrior.

Our Lord concedes you His greatest prize:
Destruction in battle, holy consumption
In truth, you've toiled well…It's yours,
The good, sweet, precious death.

Indeed you did not die in vain.
Was your death unfruitful
And without great honor?
Who has been laurelled
With well-deserved glory?
Forever you'll live…joyful, content,
There beside our ladies,
Those warrior princesses.

Farewell, my daughter, my child!
Go to them, join them:
Let them receive you and take you in.
With them, bring joy, shout praises
To our Mother and Father, the Sun—
Be with them always,
Rejoicing at His side
As He slips down the sky.

My youngest child, my beloved daughter,
My Lady—
You escape leaving us behind,
You escape kicking us aside,
We old men and women.

Was it you who wished this?
You were summoned, you were called.
So what can we do?
In your absence, here below you,
Our ruin looms!
And what is left for us?
Doomed to poverty
And the miserable existence
Of old men and women,
We will waste away
At the walls of strangers,
Huddled in the corners
Of unknown houses.

Dear Lady, please think of us,
Remember our misfortune.
It's like we can see it...
It's like we're imprisoned
Here on this earth.

In truth, we're crushed
By the heat of the sun
And the cold, biting wind.
Withering, trembling,
Covered with grime,
Our guts empty, suffering,
There is nothing we can do.
Please think of us,
Priceless daughter,
Cuauhcihuatl,
Warrior princess.

There Beyond you are happy,
In the good place,
The sweet land,
You live.
There beside
Our Lord
You live.

You now see Him face-to-face,
You now speak to Him in person...
Intercede for us!
Appeal to Him
On our behalf!

But that is enough.
We leave it in your hands.

From *First Memoranda*. The following poem is in reality a merging of two separate hymns in honor of Huitzilopochtli, the Mexica god of war, who led them out of Aztlan and set them over the other nations of Mexico, according to legend.

Song of Huitzilopochtli and His Mother

On the shield
The maiden grows big
With child.
She gives birth
At the call to arms.

In Coatepec,
Among the hills,
The divine warrior
Smears his face with paint
And seizes his shield.

No one dares
To stand against him.
The very earth trembles
As he smears his face with paint
And seizes his shield.

"I am Huitzilopochtli:
I travel the sky.
No man is my equal.
Not in vain did I don
The cape of yellow plumes—
I am the reason
The sun still shines."

A fearsome omen,
He falls on the Mixteca,
The Picha-Huasteca,
Slicing off their feet,
And then he is gone.

Oh, the ramparts
Of Tlaxotlan:
Funereal feathers
Are handed round.
Like a whirlwind he comes
To give the call to arms,
The one I name my god—
We call him Tepanquizqui:
He Who Makes War.

He is terrified,
That Tlaxotec warrior,
The dust,
The dust,
It wraps him round.

That Tlaxotec warrior,
Sore afraid—
The dust,
The dust,
Swirls all about.

"The Amanteca are our foes—
Come rally round my shield!
We fight them in their very homes—
Come rally round my shield!

"The Pipiteca are our foes—
Come rally round my shield!
We fight them in their very homes—
Come rally round my shield!"

This poem is from *Codex Chimalpopoca*. The Nahuas believed that the creator god Quetzalcoatl had ruled as a man ages earlier in the legendary city of Tollan or Tula. The king earned the anger of his priests by outlawing human sacrifice. Chief among his enemies was the dark mage Tezcatlipoca, an incarnation of Quetzalcoatl's own divine brother. With his peers, Tezcatlipoca conspired to make the king abdicate. With a magic mirror, he convinced Quetzalcoatl he was hideous and needed to hide himself beneath a mask and feathered garments. Then the sorcerer got the king and his sister drunk, causing them to violate their religious beliefs in some way (perhaps though incest). Stricken with grief, Quetzalcoatl abandoned the city, traveling for many years and impacting many lives until he finally found the place from which he would depart. Legend claimed that one day he would return to reclaim Mexico and impose a golden age of peace.

Quetzalcoatl Departs

They say that when the Feathered One
Arrived at the water, the edge of the sea,
He stopped and wept, arranged his clothes,
Strapped on his shield, his turquoise mask.
And when he was fully prepared,
He set himself ablaze, let fire eat his flesh.
Hence the name of that land, Tlatlayan,
"Place of the Burning,"
Where Quetzalcoatl self-immolated.

They say that when he was burning,
His ashes lifted up into the air—
In that cloud appeared many rare birds,
Spinning upwards through the sky:
Fire-red swans, blue cotingas,
Tzinizcans, Great White Herons,
Yellow-headed parakeets, scarlet macaws,
White-bellied parrots, and other precious birds.

Finally the wind had blown his ashes far,
And behold! The heart of Quetzalcoatl
Leapt up from the ground and hurtled to the sky!
The elders say it became the Morning Star:

Venus appeared for the very first time
After the death of the Feathered One.
Tlahuizcalpantecuhtli they called him—
Lord of the Dawn.
But first, they say, when he died,
He disappeared for four whole days,
Slipping down to the Land of the Dead,
Shadowy Mictlan.

During another four whole days
He made himself many arrows
With which to punish sin.

At the end of those eight days,
A magnificent star began to gleam—
The people named it Quetzalcoatl,
Sure that their earthly king
Had returned to his heavenly throne.

Quetzalcoatl

Poems from *Songs of Dzitbalché*

For Travelers on the Road Just Before Daybreak

You coo your song, white-winged dove,
In the branches of the ceiba tree.
With you sing the squirrel cuckoo,
The red-winged blackbird,
The lesser roadrunner
And the mockingbird.
All of them jubilant,
The Father's pets,
Delight of God.

Likewise the Mother
Has her birds:
Turtle-doves,
Little cardinals,
Euphonias
And hummingbirds.
These are her companions,
The birds of the Mother,
Our Lady.

If there is such joy
Among these creatures,
Why don't our hearts
Also feel delight?
They act this way
Each daybreak:
Beautiful ecstasy.
Just songs, just games
Enter their thoughts.

(Songs of Dzitbalché 14)

A Flower Song for Maidens Coming of Age

The beautiful, beautiful moon
Has risen above the woods,
Tracing her bright path
Across the heavens.
Suspended, she pours light
Upon the woods,
The earth entire.

A breeze blows sweetly,
Carrying perfumed scents.
The moon reaches her zenith--
Her glow silvering the world.
Joy sings out
Within every good man.

We reach the center,
The womb of the forest:
Utter stillness.
No one will see
What we have come to do.

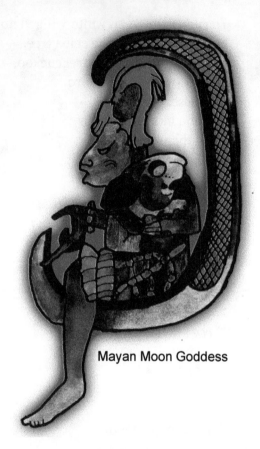

Mayan Moon Goddess

We have brought flowers:
Oleander blooms,
Ebony blossoms,
Milkwood buds.
We have brought copal incense
And wild bamboo;
A tortoise shell
And crystal dust;
New cotton thread
And spindles;
A large, fantastic flint
and a counterweight;
New needlework
and a sacrificial bird.

New sandals, too...
Everything new,
Even the thongs we use
To tie our hair back
So the old woman,
Teacher and guide,
Can anoint our necks with nectar
As she instructs us
In the ways of women.

"We stand at the heart
Of the forest,
Beside the stone pool,
Waiting for Venus,
The smoking star,
To glimmer
Above the trees.
Remove your clothes.
Let down your hair.
Bask in the moonlight,
Naked as the day of your birth,
Virgins,
Maidens,
Women."

(Songs of Dzitbalché 7)

"Receiving the flower" is a Mayan kenning for marriage.

Let's Go Receive the Flower

Happiness,
That's why we sing,
For we're off at last
To Receive the Flower.

See all the young virgins
Cheeks glowing with laughter
While innocent hearts leap
From inside their breasts.
Why are they giddy?
They know it is time
To surrender virginity
To those whom they love.

Sing the flower of love!
You'll be accompanied
By the officer of the feast
And the chief of the town,
Standing on the platform.

The chief begins to sing:
"Let's go, Let's go!
We put our wills
Before the Virgin,
The beautiful Virgin,
Queen of the Moon,
Bloom among women,
Enthroned on high.

"The Lady Christ Mary,
The Goddess Zuhuy Kaak,
Virgin Fire of the Moon,
As well as lovely Ix Kanleox,
Lady of the Precious Maize,
The beautiful one who shakes the rattle,
And the gorgeous amphibian rain spirit,
Haughty and pure.

"All of these goddesses
Fill life with goodness
Throughout the region:
Across the plains,
To the land that surrounds
And in the mountains beyond."

Come, come,
Let's go, my young friends!
Let's give one another
Such marvelous joy
Here in the town
Of Dzitbalché.

(Songs of Dzitbalché 4)

To Kiss Your Lips by the Wooden Fencepost

Wear your finest clothes—
Your day of joy has come.
Comb the sleepy tangles
From your long, black hair.

Show off that pretty skirt,
Slip on your dainty shoes.
Let long pendants dangle
From both your perfect ears.

On your shoulders a sturdy rebozo,
Garlands round your shapely neck,
Glittering bands should lovingly clasp
Both your shapely arms.

You must dazzle them, more gorgeous
Than any other woman
In this town, the seat
Of Dzitbalché.

My beauty, I love you
And I love it when they stare,
For you are utterly enchanting,
Like Venus, the Smoking Star—
Even the moon and wildflowers
Hunger for a glimpse.

Pure and perfectly white
Is your huipil blouse, my girl.
So go spread the joy of your laughter
And fill your heart with good:
Today is a time of rejoicing
For all who placed their faith in you.

(Songs of Dzitbalché 15)

Dawning of the Festive Day
Sung by the troubadour.

For the villagers,
The day becomes divine, festive—
The light of the sun begins to arise
There at the rim of the sky.
It goes and goes:
To the south as to the north,
To the east as to the west.

Tentative light comes over the earth,
Dispelling darkness.
Roaches and crickets and fleas
And fluttering nocturnal moths
Rush off to their nests in fear
Of chachalacas and pigeons,
Turtle doves and partridges,
Little pheasants, crows and mockingbirds,
While red ants rush about busy.
These wild birds begin their song
For dew gives birth to happiness.

Venus, the beautiful star,
Shimmers over the trees,
Smoking as it dips down the sky,
And the moon fades to nothing
Above the green expanse of forest.

The holiday begins,
Bringing joy to our village,
For the sun, renewed,
Has come to illuminate the lives
Of all the souls who live united
Here, in our village.

(*Songs of Dzitbalché* 11)

This is a song for greeting the new year.

Dowsing Old Man Fire on the Mountaintop

The sun is snatched by the smoking star
There in the west at the rim of the sky.
The tunkul drums begin to thrum,
The conch horn shrilly sounds,
The zacatan tattoos a beat,
While the gourd pipe
Sings a melody
So that everyone
Who hears the tune
Will come assemble here.

Running and jumping
They arrive before the popolna,
The meeting house of the town
Where the Lord Serpent Bishop waits.
There, too, are the governor and rain priests,
The chief of the town and his aides.
Expectant stand the musicians,
The singers, actors, dancers,
Contortionists, and acrobats,
Hunchbacked dwarves
And spectators.

Everyone has come following
The Lord Serpent Bishop,
Eager to be entertained
By the grand spectacle
That will soon take place
In the very center
Of our town square.

As the sun is pulled down
Past the rim of the sky,

The ceremony begins.
Copal incense fills the air—
The Lord of Heaven
Draws the smoke from the fire,
Using it to darken the face
Of our Father, the Sun.

Let us go! Let us go to the trunk
Of the holy ceiba tree!
Let us leave an offering there
To greet the new year!
We made it!
The five poisonous days
Have come and gone.
Let us join together
In the town,
And then at its eastern edge
Let us lift the wooden pole
Upon the ridge
In honor of Old Man Fire.

Bring   out   the   new,
Throw   out   the   old.
Father God permits us
To pass the black days
At the end of the year
Together here in town,
For there will come other days,
Other months,
Other years,
Other generations.

At the entrance to the town
Let us place a new end stone.
Let us look for a pure white stone
To mark the passing
Of another year.

(*Songs of Dzitbalché* 12)

An Orphan's Sad Lament, Sung to the Beat of a Drum

I was just a little boy
When my mother died,
When my father died.
Oh, Lord...Oh, Lord.

I was left in the hands
And hearts of my friends,
I have no one on earth.
Oh, Lady....Oh, Lord.

Two days had passed
When my friends all died:
I was left on my own in the dark,
Oh, groping along in the night.

When that day had passed
That I was left all alone,
A stranger came and took me
By the hand to his home.

Oh, Lord...Oh, Lord...
Oh, Lady...Oh, Lord!

A truly evil man was he
And many bad things
He did to me:
Don't think I'll ever stop weeping.

No relatives, I'm all alone,
Shuffling through my land.
Weeping day and night
Consumes my eyes and soul.

Oh, such evil weighs me down!
Lord, take pity on your child!
Put an end to my suffering
Through death or righteous soul!

Oh, Lord...My beautiful Lord.
Poor little orphan boy,
Groping and alone,
Goes from door to door,

Begging scraps of pity.
May everyone that sees him
Give him loving kindness!
He has no home or clothes,
He doesn't have a fire.

Oh, Lord...My beautiful Lord.
Please take pity on me,
Make mine a righteous soul
So that I can find the courage
To ease the orphan's pain.

(*Songs of Dzitbalché* 8)

Amidst the Ruins

It's vital we never lose count
Of how many long generations
Have passed since the faraway age
When here in this land lived
Great and powerful men
Who lifted the walls of those cities—
The ancient, awesome ruins
That dot the plains of the Yucatán,
Pyramids rising like hills.

We try to determine their meaning
Here in our humbler towns,
A meaning that matters today,
One we draw from the signs
Those men of the Golden Age—
Men of this land, our forefathers—
Urged us to seek in the sky.

Consecrated to this task,
We turn our faces upward
As darkness slowly falls
From zenith to horizon
And fills the sky with stars
In which we scry our fate.

(*Songs of Dzitbalché* 5)

This is a tale from the age of Lord Rattlesnake and the Feathered Serpent.

The Parable of Lord Centipede

I have come to tell you, my fellows,
Of a time when here
In this region, these plains,
This broad Yucatan
Dwelled ancient giants
And hunchbacked dwarves.
No human being like you or me
Had ever arrived in these lands.

For many, many years
Lord Centipede with his seven heads
Strode up and down the plains alone.
If you saw him suddenly cross your path,
It was to devour you
Or to trouble your life
Should you not understand
What he asked of you.

But, behold, the day arrived
When there was one
Who could respond—
Not a giant or dwarf,
But a man.

When he heard the answered words
Lord Centipede raged and raged
Because the man who could respond
To what he asked
Had to be Lord Centipede, too!

How else could a being understand
And respond to that seven-fold mind?

Thus was he seized by this evil lie
Which he began to believe and repeat,
Having been deceived in his pride
By the human response.

(Songs of Dzitbalché 10)

Cizin was the Mayan god of the underworld, unleashed at the end of every year for five days.

Prayer to the Sun

Dedicated to the great lords: the chief of the town of Dzitbalché and the governor of Campeche.

I am come.
I am come to where
Your tall tree stands,
To earn your joy,
My lovely Lord.

It is you who bestows
Everything good,
All the blessings
That lie in your hand.

Grant me your blessings,
Your redeeming word.

I can see
What is good
What is bad
In this world.

Grant me your light,
You, my true father.

Grant me great understanding
In my thoughts and my reason
So I may bow my head to you
Forever and ever.

Lift the spell of pain from me
That the demon Cizin cast.

If what I swear is not true,
Let my mother die,
Let my father die,
Let my wife die,
Let my livestock die,
If what I tell you, Father,
Is not true.

I implore you,
Beautiful Heavenly Father,
Glorious upon your throne
On high.

Therefore do I bow to you,
Blessed and only God,
You who grant the good
And the bad on this earth:

I call out to you...

(*Songs of Dzitbalché* 2)

Hunabku or One God is a name that was likely not used before the Conquest.

Prayer to the Father, Who Holds the Years in His Hand

Father mine, I come before you,
Forehead bowed, eyes cast down.
Nine days have passed
Since I touched or looked upon a woman.
Nor I have I let evil thoughts
Fester in my mind.

Though poor, I come
With my new pants,
With my new tunic.
Also, as you can see,
Father mine,
I seek not the evil of sin
Before your face,
My true Father,
Hunabku,
The Only God.

Thus in simple purity,
My soul aglow,
I come to see you
In your holy place,
Surrendering my thought
And will to you
Here on this earth.

You,
O Magnificent Sun,
Shower good things
On all living creatures
Here on this earth.

You
Provide for our needs,
You hold this world
Where all men live
In the palm of your hand.

You
Are the true redeemer
Who grants the good.

(Songs of Dzitbalché 6)

This piece was intoned every month by the shaman.

Prayer to the God of Medicine

I, the shaman and curandero,
Intone the monthly prayer
So there will be
Pomolche' in the forests,
Bastard cherry in the woods.
So that fast will cling the roots
Of the bacalche' and Spanish elm.

In the east as in the north,
In the west as in the south,
He comes down the four branches
Of the celestial road
That leads to the house
Where stands the mat,
From which He rules,
The wise Hunabku,
Judging every man.

He ensures food and life
For anyone who would dedicate
His spirit to study the things of this earth.
He grants health to such a person
For he is Lord
Of fire
Of water
Of air
Of earth:
Lord of this world,
Of all that He made.

Lord Hunabku apportions
The good and the bad
To good and bad souls

Because He is who
Brings light to the earth,
Because He is the Father.
He holds it all in the palm of His hand:
The sun and the moon,
Venus, the smoking star, bright bloom of heaven,
The clouds and the rain,
Lightning bolts and swarms of gnats,
The beasts of the field and birds of the air...
Everything in the palm of His hand.

(*Songs of Dzitbalché* 9)

Sacrificial Victim

To a Sacrificial Victim at the Dance of Kolomché

Sturdy, athletic youths,
Hardened veterans of the shield:
They make their way to the heart
Of our sacred town square,
Eager to measure their might
In the Dance of Kolomché—
Rite of Little Arrows.

In the midst of their striving, a man—
Bound to a pillar of stone,
Smeared with that beautiful indigo.
Wreaths of purple balché flowers
Have been draped around his neck,
Blooms placed in both his hands,
Blossoms wrapped about his feet,
His limbs redolent of perfume.

Lift your spirits, beautiful man—
Let pride swell the heart our arrows will pierce.
You will soon see the face of our Father the Sun
And remain with him on high, never returning
Jade-feathered like the little hummingbird
Or dressed in the skin of the mighty stag,
The night-dark jaguar, the tropical mockingbird,
Or the Great Curassow—golden-beaked, sable-plumed.

Lift your spirits! Be of good cheer!
Think of naught but your Father.
No evil will be done to you.
Remember the beautiful virgins
That followed your journey from town to town...
Show no fear. Open your soul
To what will soon befall you.

Here comes the great Lord Governor;
He has brought the chief of the town
As well as the Lord Serpent Bishop.
At their side you see a proud officer from Aké,
Accompanied by his deputy... Smile!
You should feel very proud
For you are the only one chosen
To be the voice of your community
There before our Glorious Lord,
Who was set above the earth in ages past,
And etched your fate into trees and stones.

(*Songs of Dzitbalché* 1)

The Dance of the Archer

Scouts, scouts in the trees—
Once, twice...
Let us hunt at the edge of the wood,
Dancing as we run
Three circuits roundabout.

Lift your head,
Narrow your eyes,
Make no mistake
So you hit your mark.

Your arrow is sharp
Your bowstring is taut
You used good resin
To glue fast the fletchings
Close to the nock.

You have smeared yourself well
With fat from a buck:
Your biceps, your thighs,
Your knees and your testicles,
Your ribs and your chest.

Make three running turns
Round that pillar of stone
Where that manly youth,
That pure and virgin man,
Has been bound.

Make the first turn.
Upon the second,
Seize your bow,
Notch your shaft,
Aim for his chest.

No need to use
All your strength,
To fly your arrow
To its mark.
Do not sink your barb
Too deep in his flesh.
His strength must fail him
Bit by bit—
Just as our beautiful Father,
God, has ordained.

Yes, at the second turn round
That blue pillar of stone,
Let your arrow fly,
And at the next turn,
Shoot him once again.

All this you must do
Without pausing your dance,
As do all good squires and soldiers,
Men selected to please the eyes of God.

For this is how we call the sun
To rise above the eastern woods.
Hear the song of the archer begin—
The squires and soldiers
Give their all.

(*Songs of Dzitbalché* 13)

The Mayans established two different calendars, one with 260 days and one with 365. The latter was divided into eighteen months of twenty days, which left five days orphaned at the end of the solar year. These were called the "Wayeb," and evil was said to be loosed upon humanity during that brief week.

Wayeb

Five black days
That poison the year:
Monstrous days,
A time for laments.

Lord Cizin is loosed
From his underworld realm.
He unleashes evil,
And no one may stop him.
Goodness is gone,
Leaving groans and cries.

Eighteen months
Of twenty days—
One whole year
Is named and closed.

Now it begins:
The nameless week.
Sorrowful nights
Of sinister black.

There's no gorgeous glow
From the eye of God
For His children below
On forsaken earth.

During five days
He measures the sins
Of every human:

Woman and man,
Great and small,
Rich and poor,
Foolish and wise.

From the Lord Serpent bishop
To the chief of the town,
His deputies, officers,
Sheriff and councilors,
Priests of the rain god:
Every last man.

All our transgressions
Are measured these days
For the time will come
They will mark the end
Of the world in flame.

Hence the need
For a careful count
Of human crimes.
To accomplish this task
He molded a jar
Of tree-termite clay.

And there He deposits
Every last tear
Wept for the evils
We do in this world.

When it's filled to the brim,
Everything ends.

(*Songs of Dzitbalché* 3)

Glossary

Acamapichtli—first ruler of the Mexica in Tenochtitlan

Acolhua—a Nahua nation that arrived in the Valley of Mexico around 1200 CE. Part of the Aztec Triple Alliance. Capital city was Texcoco, a cultural center for the region.

Acolmiztli—the second name of *Nezahualcoyotl,* poet and ruler of Texcoco.

Aké—a pre-Colombian Mayan city in Yucatan.

Amanteca—the people of Amantlan, known for their feather-working skill. Originally enemies of the Mexica, they were absorbed into the Triple Alliance and became a special guild of workers.

Amaquemeca—a loose confederation of Chichimec villages conquered by the Triple Alliance in 1465. Its inhabitants helped the Spaniards overthrow Tenochtitlan.

Anahuac—"by the waters," a Nahua term for the Basin of Mexico (and by extension for Tenochtitlan or the Triple Alliance).

Aquiauhtzin—a nobleman and poet from the town of Ayapanco in the Chalco region, a tributary kingdom of the Aztec Triple Alliance.

Atl tlachinolli—"water burned-thing" or *deluge and conflagration.* A Nahuatl kenning for "war."

Atlixco—a Chichimec region, tributary of Huexotzinco, where many flower wars were fought

Axaycatl—father of Moctezuma II. He assumed the throne at age 18 and died when he was 30, inspiring generations of songwriters.

Ayapanco—a town in the Chalco region.

Ayocuan—prince of Tecamachalco, a Chichimec kingdom conquered by the Aztec Triple Alliance in the late 15th century.

Azcapotzalco—capital of the Tepanec empire, which opposed the hegemony of the Triple Alliance until 1428, when the city fell to Aztec forces.

Aztecs—"people of Aztlan." This term is best understood as referring to all the Nahua nations constituting or allied with the Triple Alliance, though it is also used as a synonym of Mexica, the empire's dominant group

Aztlan—a mythological region in the north from which the Nahua tribes were believed to have emigrated in the distant past. The Mexica, led by Huitzilopochtli, were the last to leave, according to the legends, and so when they arrived in the Valley of Mexico, all the land was already taken.

Bacalché—a flowering tree native to Yucatan (Bourreria pulchra).

Balché—type of purple flower found in Yucatan.

Cacamatl—last king of Texcoco, son of Nezahualpilli. Also known by the honorific Cacamatzin. Captured, tortured and killed by the Spanish in 1520.

Cahualtzin—cousin of Moctezuma I, leader in the wars with Chalco.

Calpan—a small pueblo associated with Huexotzinco (and therefore an enemy of the Triple Alliance).

Chalco—a tributary of the Aztec Triple Alliance that allied with the Spanish during the Conquest.

Chamotzin—"dark red feather," a term used to call upon the spirit of a woman who has just passed away.

Chicomoztoc—"place of seven caves." Mythical place of origin for the seven original Nahua tribes, probably adopted from existing Mesoamerican religions, many of which also make reference to such a region. Emerging from those caves, the tribes settled in Aztlan.

Cihuacoatl—a goddess of midwifery and childbirth who helped Quetzalcoatl create human beings. Often depicted with a spear and shield, as childbirth was likened to war.

Cihuateotl (plural *cihuateteo*)—"deified woman," the soul of a mother who has died during childbirth. The cihuateteo emerged from their paradise in the West every evening to accompany the sun as it slid down the western sky to the Underworld. It was important to revere these spirits correctly, as they were known to haunt crossroads and steal children if ritual was neglected.

Cihuapipiltin—"princesses," an epithet for the *cihuateteo*.

Cizin—the Mayan god of the underworld, unleashed at the end of every year for five days.

Coatepec—"serpent mountain," the birthplace of the god Huitzil-opochtli.

Cuatlecoatl—the son of Acamapichtli, first ruler of Tenochtitlan. He served as a *tēuctlahtoh* or duke during the reign of his half-brother Huitzilihhuitl and was later given the rank of *tlacochcalcatl* or commanding general. His nephews were Moctezuma I and Tlacaelel.

Cuauhcihuatl—"strong woman," an epithet of certain goddesses and women who have died in childbirth.

Cuecuextzin—"jewled armband," a term used to call upon the spirit of a man who has just passed away.

Cuitlizcatl—Tlaxcalan prince who aided the Spaniards against Tenochtitlan.

Curandero—Spanish word used to translate the Mayan *tz'ac yah*, "medicine man."

Eagle warriors/knights—*cuauhtmeh,* a special order of infantry soldier in the Aztec army.

Ehcatepec—an Aztec city-state.

Ehecatl—the wind god, a manifestation of Quetzalcoatl.

Giver of Life—*Ipalnemoani*, "he through whom everything lives," an epithet of the god Tezcatlipoca.

House of Holy Writ—Aztec philosophy saw the earth as a book (or series of books) written and illustrated by the Giver of Life (like their own *amoxtli* or papyrus codices). The dwelling place of this divine author is often called *amoxcalli*, the house of *amoxtli*, which I have translated as *holy writ* to differentiate between the creations of man and god.

House of Spring—another epithet of Tamoanchan or Tonatiuhchan.

Huastec—an indigenous people of Mexico that split off from the Mayans some three millennia before the arrival of the Nahua tribes

Huexotzinco—Chichimec city-state independent of Aztec rule.

Hunabku—"one god," a Mayan title for the supreme being.

Itzpapalotl—a fierce goddess associated with the souls of mothers who die in childbirth and of children who die as infants.

Itztompatepec—Chalcan city destroyed by the Triple Alliance.

Ix Kanleox—Mayan goddess of fertility and agriculture.

Jaguar warriors/knights—*ocelomeh*, a special order of infantry soldier in the Aztec army.

Kolomché—Mayan "rite of little arrows," in which a victim is sacrificed to the sun.

Lord of the Near and the Nigh—*Tloqueh Nahuaqueh*, an epithet of the god Tezcatlipoca.

Macuilxochitl—daughter of Tlacaelel. Only female Aztec poet whose work survives.

Mage—used to translate the word *nahualli*, a sort of legendary shape-shifting sorcerer.

Malinalco—a tributary nation of the Triple Alliance populated mainly by Matlanzincas.

Matlanzinca—1. the people of the Valley of Toluca or its capital city; 2. adjective describing anything from this region.

Matlanzinco—the Valley of Toluca or its capital city, conquered by the Aztecs around 1476 CE.

Mexica—a Nahua people who immigrated to central Mexico around 1248 CE. After being variously expelled and assimilated by other Nahua nations in the Valley of Mexico, the Mexica in 1325 CE founded the city of Tenochtitlan on an island in Lake Texcoco. Fifty years later, their first king was selected. The Mexica were a tributary of Azcapotzalco for another fifty years until King Itzcoatl allied with Nezahualcoyotl, the exiled king of Texcoco, to defeat their Tepanec overlords. This alliance was strengthened by Moctezuma I and Tlacaelel, who reshaped religion, history and government, creating a common mythological heritage for the Nahuas and establishing the flower wars.

Mexico—another name for Tenochtitlan, city-state of the Mexica.

Mictlan—the Underworld in Nahua religion, to which most people were destined upon death. There they would face a four-year journey of trials before finding eternal rest. Also known as *Ximoayan*.

Mixcoatl Camaxtli—patron god of Huexotzinco. A hunting deity.

Mixteca—"cloud people," an indigenous Mexican people.

Mocihuaquetzque—"those who arise as women," an epithet of the *cihuateteo*.

Moctezuma I—ruler of Tenochtitlan after his uncle, Itzcoatl. One of the main architects of the Triple Alliance.

Moctezuma II—king of Tenochtitlan and emperor of the Triple Alliance when the Spaniards arrived in Mexico.

Monkey scribes—Hun Batz and Hun Chuen, patron gods for the Mayans of writing, dance, painting and mathematics. The two are inversions of the Mayan hero twins (their younger brothers Hunahpu and Xbalanque, who descended into the Underworld to rescue their father). Also twin brothers, the scribes are the elder sons of Hun Hunahpu (the resurrected maize god). The scribes were turned into monkeys by their younger brothers, whom they continually tormented until having the tables turned on them.

Moyocoyatzin—"Self-maker," a title given both to Tezcatlipoca, the capricious supreme deity of the Aztecs, and to Ometeotl, the divine duality.

Nahua—a group of peoples who emigrated from the deserts of northern Mexico and the US Southwest into central Mexico over several centuries beginning about 400 CE.

Nahui Ollin—"four movement," the fifth and present age in Aztec cosmology, so named for the calendar day on which it began. The glyph for this day, featuring a solar eye from which rays of light shine, was carved into Aztec war drums and represented the dynamic rhythms of the universe.

Nezahualcoyotl— a poet-king of Texcoco under whom the arts flourished. Nicknamed Yoyontzin. Allied with Tenochtitlan against Azcapotzalco.

Nezahualpilli—liberal-minded ruler of Texcoco, son of Nezahualcoyotl.

Nonohualco—a term used to describe a place where one language ends and another begins; borderland; far-off place.

Ocuillan—a city-state valuable because of the trade routes that passed through it.

Ohuaya—one of several "nonsense" words (typically not translated) scattered throughout Nahuatl verse. They are apparently meant to express moments of divinely inspired ecstasy, and they may have helped bards fit a line of poetry to a particular beat.

Ometeotl—"the god of duality," highest divinity in Aztec religion, which embraced both halves of dualities: both the feminine and the masculine, as well as light-dark, positive-negative, spirit-matter, etc. All Nahua gods can be seen as facets or emanations of Ometeotl.

Omeyocan—"the place of duality," the thirteenth and highest of heavens in Aztec religion, cosmic origin of all things.

Otomi—an indigenous Mexican people, likely the original inhabitants of the Valley of Mexico before Nahua immigration. Because of their reputation as fierce warriors, the Aztec army created an elite military order named after the aboriginal group.

Picha-huasteca—an indigenous Mexican people that lived along the coast of the Gulf of Mexico.

Pipiteca—an unidentified group, possibly an indigenous tribe later absorbed into Aztec society like the Amanteca.

Place of the Shorn—*Ximoayan*, the afterlife, used to refer to Mictlan or any destination of the human soul.

Pomolché—a tall tree native to Yucatan (*jatropha gaumeri*).

Popolna—the meeting house of a Mayan town.

Quecehuatl—an epithet of Tecayehuatzin, ruler of Huexotzinco.

Quetzal—brightly colored birds of the trogon family. The long wing and tail feathers of the Resplendent Quetzal were highly valued in Nahua culture.

Quetzalcoatl—"feathered serpent," brother of Tezcatlipoca. A creator god responsible for bringing humanity into existence, he was either incarnated as or confused with the ruler of Tollan who tried to outlaw human sacrifice and who was raised into the sky as Venus after his immolation.

Quilaztli—a powerful sorceress in Aztec mythology who remained with a portion of the Mexica in Aztlan. She is associated with the goddess Cihuacoatl.

Rebozo—Spanish word used to translate the Mayan *ooch'*, cape or scarf.

Roseate spoonbill—*quechol,* a wading bird that resembles a flamingo with a shorter neck and a spoon-shaped bill.

Tamoanchan—an ill-defined paradise from which the first humans emerged, often used synonymously with the 13-tiered heaven or with Tonatiuhchan.

Tecamachalco—a Chichimec kingdom conquered by the Aztec Triple Alliance in the late 15th century.

Tecayehuatzin—a philosopher-poet who ruled in the Chichimec city-state of Huexotzinco.

Techotlala—grandfather of Acolmiztli.

Tecualoyan—"place of the man-eating beasts," an Otomi city.

Temilotzin—poet and friend of Cuauhtemoc, the last Aztec emperor, who leapt into the sea (and to his certain death) rather than be taken to Spain to die in that distant country.

Tenochtitlan—Mexico, city of the Mexica, founded on an islet in the midst of Lake Texcoco.

Teteoinnan—mother of the gods, also called Tlalli Iyollo, "Heart of the Earth."

Tepanecapan—region of central Mexico controlled by the Tepaneca.

Tepanquizqui—"he who makes war," an epithet of Huitzilopochtli.

Tezcatlipoca—a creator god associated with jaguars, magic, darkness, rulership, strife and violence. Tezcatlipoca was feared and reverenced, and the Nahuas had many names for him, including *Titlacahuan* (We Are His Slaves), *Ipalnemoani* (Giver of Life), *Necoc Yaotl* (Enemy on Both Sides), *Tloqueh Nahuaqueh* (Lord of the Near and the Nigh) and *Moquequeloa* (The Mocker). Much of the verse in compiled in *Songs of Mexico* and *Ballads of the Lords of New Spain* was likely originally addressed to him.

Tezozomoc—long-lived Tepanec ruler of Azcapotzalco.

Tilma—outer garment or cape worn by Aztec men.

Tlacaelel—brother of Chimalpopoca and Moctezuma I, who as advisor to four consecutive kings retooled the mythology of the Nahua peoples, enhancing the role of the Mexica, elevating Huitzilopochtli to the chief spot in the pantheon, increasing the number of human sacrifices and instituting the flower wars.

Tlacahuepan—*younger* brother of Moctezuma II, a *tlacochcalcatl* or high general of the Aztec army who died during a flower war with Huexotzinco, becoming a symbol of heroism in battle.

Tlacotepec—a city in Matlatzinco.

Tlacochcalcatl—military title: one of two high generals in the Aztec army. He would lead the forces of the Triple Alliance into battle, and he was responsible for the four main armories of Tenochtitlan.

Tlahuizcalpantecuhtli—"lord of the dawn," an epithet of Quetzalcoatl.

Tlaltecatl/Tlaltecatzin—the first king of Texcoco, an Acolhuan city-state that under his rule became a center of culture and wisdom.

Tlatlayan—"place of the burning," where Quetzalcoatl immolated himself.

Tlaltecuhtli—a primeval leviathan-like earth goddess.

Tlaxcala—Chichimec city-state.

Tlaxotlan—a district within the city of Tenochtitlan.

Tlilat—an Otomi warrior who wounded Axaycatl.

Toci—"our grandmother," an epithet of Teteoinnan.

Tollan—also Tula. The legendary city in which Quetzalcoatl ruled.

Toluca—name of the valley also called Matlatzinco.

Tonatiuh—Aztec sun god, often merged with Huitzilopochtli.

Tonatiuhchan— the House of the Sun, a paradise that awaits warriors killed in combat or sacrificed.

Totoquihuaztl—poet and ruler of Tlacopan, one of the three city-states in the Aztec Triple Alliance.

Tunkul—long, u-shaped Mayan drum.

Tzinizcan—the mountain trogon, a species native to Mexico, Honduras and Guatemala. The bird's plumage is mostly green, though it sports a bright red breast and a white band around its throat.

Unknowable Realm—*Quenonamican*, "place of the unknown." The afterlife.

Wayeb—five unlucky days at the end of the Mayan solar calendar.

Xicotencatl—a long-lived ruler of Tizatlan, a Tlaxcalan city.

Xiquipilco—an Amaquemecan city.

Xiuhnel and Mimich—demigod brothers who chase a pair of deer fallen from heaven. When after much pursuit the deer transform into women, the brothers show them mercy. The women attempt to seduce the hunters, and Xiuhnel is eaten by one after intercourse. Mimich tries to escape the other, but she runs after him until she falls on a cactus, at which point he fills her with arrows. He then mourns the death of his brother.

Xochiyaoyotl—flower wars, arranged battles used for the acquisition of sacrificial victims.

Xocotitlan—a city in the Valley of Toluca.

Yaotzin—"Revered Enemy," an epithet of Tezcatlipoca.

Yoyontzin—nickname of Nezahualcoyotl.

Zacatan—vertical Mayan drum made from a hollowed tree trunk.

Zuhuy Kaak—Mayan goddess of virginity and fire.

Book Club Discussion Questions for
Flower, Song, Dance: Aztec and Mayan Poetry

1. Contrast the attitude toward romantic love expressed in "To Kiss Your Lips by the Wooden Fencepost" and "Ode to Fleeting Love."

2. Discuss the Aztec metaphor of god as painter/composer.

3. Based on the songs ascribed to him, explain the basic philosophy of King Nezahualcoyotl.

4. Though the state religion of the Aztec Triple Alliance taught that death in battle or sacrifice would result in a person's spending eternity in the paradise of the sun, what evidence is there in poems from *Songs of Mexico* and *Ballads of the Lords of New Spain* of philosophical doubts about the afterlife?

5. How does death impact survivors in poems such as "An Orphan's Sad Lament, Sung to the Beat of a Drum," "To a Woman Who Has Died during Childbirth," and "Moctezuma Mourns His Brother's Death?"

6. Based on the selections translated from Nahuatl, what appears to have been the general attitude of Aztec culture toward women? Does this contrast with the apparent Mayan view?

7. What sorts of things do flowers and birds appear to symbolize in Aztec culture? How does this differ from the Mayan perspective?

8. What thematic differences and similarities exist between Aztec and Mayan poems in this collection?

9. Aztec gods are often ascribed what modern readers might consider evil motivations and bad behavior. Discuss the difference between "righteous" behavior in these Mesoamerican cultures and present notions, focusing on actions that make a person worthy to enter paradise.

10. In what ways do the *Songs of Dzitbalché* serve as tools for community coherence?

Bibliography

Bierhorst, John. *Cantares Mexicanos: Songs of the Aztecs*. Stanford, CA: Stanford University Press, 1985.

Bierhorst, John. *Ballads of the Lords of New Spain: The Codex Romances de los Señores de la Nueva España*. Austin, TX: University of Texas Press, 2009.

Bolles, David. *Combined Dictionary–Concordance of the Yucatecan Mayan Language* (revised 2003). Lee, New Hampshire: Foundation for the Advancement of Mesoamerican Studies, Inc. (FAMSI), 1997.
   http://www.famsi.org/reports/96072/index.html

Bolles, David and Alejandra K. *A Grammar of the Yucatecan Mayan Language*. Revised edition. Lancaster, CA: Labyrinthos Press, 2001.

Carrasco, David. *Religions of Mesoamerica: Cosmovision and Ceremonial Centers*. Prospect Heights, IL: Waveland Press, 1990.

De la Garza Camino, Mercedes. *Literatura Maya*. Caracas: Fundación Biblioteca Ayacucho, 1980.

De Sahagún, Bernadino. *Florentine Codex: General History of the Things of New Spain, Book 6—Rhetoric and Moral Philosophy*. Trans.And Ed. Charles E. Dibble and Arthur J. O. Anderson. Santa Fe: University of Utah, 1969.

Garibay Kintana, Ángel M. *Poesía náhuatl I: Romances de los señores de la Nueva España*. Mexico City: Universidad Nacional Autónama de México, 1964.

Garibay Kintana, Ángel M. *Poesía náhuatl II: Cantares mexicanos, primera parte*. Mexico City: Universidad Nacional Autónama de México, 1965.

Garibay Kintana, Ángel M. *Poesía náhuatl II: Cantares mexicanos, segunda parte*. Mexico City: Universidad Nacional Autónama de México, 1965.

Launey, Michel. *An Introduction to Classical Nahuatl*. Trans. Christopher Mackay. Cambridge University Press, 2011.

León-Portilla, Miguel and Earl Shorris. *In the Language of Kings: An Anthology of Mesoamerican Literature, Pre-Columbian to the Present*. New York: W.W. Norton & Company, 2002.

León-Portilla, Miguel. *Fifteen Poets of the Aztec World*. Norman: University of Oklahoma Press, 1992.

Markman, Roberta H. and Peter T. Markman. *The Flayed God: the Mesoamerican Mythological Tradition*. San Francisco: Harper Collins, 1992.

Miller, Mary and Karl Taube. *An Illustrated Dictionary of the Gods and Symbols of Ancient Mexico and the Maya*. London: Thames & Hudson, 1993.

Edmonson, Munro S. *"The Songs of Dzitbalché: A Literary Commentary." Tlalocan*, 9 (1982): pp.173–208.

Sullivan, Thelma. *Scattering of Jades: Stories, Poems, and Prayers of the Aztecs*. Ed. Timothy J. Knab. Tucson: University of Arizona Press, 1994.

Printed in the USA
CPSIA information can be obtained
at www.ICGtesting.com
LVHW021817160923
758191LV00017B/1447